8.95

THE MANY FACES
OF REALISM

THE PAUL CARUS LECTURES

In Memory of
PAUL CARUS
1852–1919
Editor of *The Open Court*
1888–1919
and of *The Monist*
1890–1919
*This series published on the occasion of the Centennial of
Open Court Publishing Company*

THE MANY FACES
OF REALISM

The Paul Carus Lectures

HILARY PUTNAM

OPEN COURT
LaSalle, Illinois

OPEN COURT and the above logo are registered in the U.S. Patent and
Trademark Office.

First printing 1987.
Second printing 1989.

Printed and bound in the United States of America.

This is the twenty-fourth series of lectures to be delivered in the Paul
Carus Lecture Series and the sixteenth to be published.

Library of Congress Cataloging-in-Publication Data

Putnam, Hilary.
    The many faces of realism.

    (The Paul Carus lectures ; 16 ser. (Dec. 1985))
    Includes index.
    1. Philosophy. I. Title. II. Series: Paul Carus lectures ; 16 ser.
B29.P87   1987   149'.2   87-7817
ISBN 0-8126-9042-7
ISBN 0-8126-9043-5 (pbk.)

To the memory of my beloved uncle
PETER SAMPSON
whose help and encouragement many years ago
made possible my graduate education

CONTENTS

Preface

When I wrote *Reason, Truth and History*, I described my
purpose as breaking the stranglehold which a number of
dichotomies have on our thinking, chief among them the
dichotomy between 'objective' and 'subjective' views of
truth and reason. I described my view thus (p. xi): "I shall
advance a view in which the mind does not simply 'copy'
a world which admits description by One True Theory. But
my view is not a view in which the mind makes up the
world (or makes it up subject to constraints imposed by
'methodological canons' and mind-independent 'sense-
data'). If one must use metaphorical language, then let the
metaphor be this: the mind and the world jointly make up
the mind and the world."

The invitation to give the Paul Carus Lectures at the
December 1985 meeting of the American Philosophical
Association in Washington, D.C. provided me with the
opportunity to further specify the alternative that I see to
metaphysical realist views of reality and truth, on the one
hand, and to cultural relativist ones, on the other. In the
earlier book I described current views of truth as 'alienated'
views, views which cause one to lose one or another part
of one's self and the world; in these lectures I have tried to
elaborate on this remark, and on the connection between a
non-alienated view of truth and a non-alienated view of
human flourishing.

The custom is for the Carus Lectures to be published in
an expanded form—sometimes at many times the length of
the lectures that were actually given. Here I have tried to
stay close to my actual lectures in Washington with one
signal change; I have inserted a lecture (the present Lecture
II) which was not actually read in Washington. Keeping the
lecture format has seemed to me preferable to a rewriting

which would eliminate the actual sense of a person speaking to other persons face to face.

I am indebted to Daniel Alvarez, Thomas Carlson, Marcus Singer, and Kenneth Winkler for historical instruction and for pointing out errors. As always, I am indebted in one way or another to every one of my colleagues in the Harvard Philosophy Department. Dieter Henrich (of Harvard and Munich), whose lectures on Kant at Harvard have been an immense source of inspiration, deserves special mention. If the names of Goodman, Quine, and Rawls occur in these pages, that is only a very small indication of my debt to them. I am particularly grateful to Burton Dreben for many suggestions which I believe have improved this work. And, once again, I have to thank Ruth Anna Putnam, for much more than stimulation and advice, but certainly for that too.

Lecture I

IS THERE STILL ANYTHING TO SAY ABOUT REALITY AND TRUTH?

The man on the street, Eddington reminded us,
visualizes a table as 'solid'—that is, as *mostly* solid matter.
But physics has discovered that the table is mostly empty
space: that the distance between the particles is immense
in relation to the radius of the electron or the nucleus of
one of the atoms of which the table consists. One reaction
to this state of affairs, the reaction of Wilfrid Sellars,[1] is to
deny that there are tables at all as we ordinarily conceive
them (although he chooses an ice cube rather than a table
as his example). The commonsense conception of ordinary
middle-sized material objects such as tables and ice cubes
(the 'manifest image') is simply *false* in Sellars's view
(although not without at least some cognitive value—there
are real objects that the 'tables' and 'ice cubes' of the
manifest image 'picture', acccording to Sellars, even if
these real objects are not the layman's tables and ice
cubes). I don't agree with this view of Sellars's, but I hope
he will forgive me if I use it, or the phenomenon of its
appearance on the philosophical scene, to highlight certain
features of the philosophical debate about 'realism'.

First of all, this view illustrates the fact that Realism
with a capital 'R' doesn't always deliver what the innocent
expect of it. If there is any appeal of Realism which is
wholly legitimate it is the appeal to the commonsense
feeling that *of course* there are tables and chairs, and any
philosophy that tell us that there really aren't—that there

are really only sense data, or only 'texts', or whatever, is more than slightly crazy. In appealing to this commonsense feeling, Realism reminds me of the Seducer in the old-fashioned melodrama. In the melodramas of the 1890s the Seducer always promised various things to the Innocent Maiden which he failed to deliver when the time came. In this case the Realist (the evil Seducer) promises common sense (the Innocent Maiden) that he will rescue her from her enemies (Idealists, Kantians and Neo-Kantians, Pragmatists, and the fearsome self-described "Irrealist" Nelson Goodman) who (the Realist says) want to deprive her of her good old ice cubes and chairs. Faced with this dreadful prospect, the fair Maiden naturally opts for the company of the commonsensical Realist. But when they have travelled together for a little while the 'Scientific Realist' breaks the news that what the Maiden is going to get *isn't* her ice cubes and tables and chairs. In fact, all there *really* is—the Scientific Realist tells her over breakfast—is what 'finished science' will say there is— whatever that may be. She is left with a promissory note for She Knows Not What, and the assurance that even if there *aren't* tables and chairs, still there are some *Dinge an sich* that her 'manifest image' (or her 'folk physics', as some Scientific Realists put it) 'picture'. Some will say that the lady has been had.

Thus, it is clear that the name 'Realism' can be claimed by or given to at least two very different philosophical attitudes (and, in fact, to many). The philosopher who claims that only scientific objects 'really exist' and that much, if not all, of the commonsense world is mere 'projection' claims to be a 'realist', but so does the philosopher who insists that there *really are* chairs and ice cubes (and some of these ice cubes really are *pink*), and these two attitudes, these two images of the world, can lead to and have led to many different programs for philosophy.

Husserl[2] traces the first line of thought, the line that denies that there 'really are' commonsense objects, back to

Galileo, and with good reason. The present Western world-
view depends, according to Husserl, on a new way of
conceiving 'external objects'— the way of mathematical
physics. An external thing is conceived of as a congeries of
particles (by atomists) or as some kind of extended
disturbance (in the seventeenth century, a 'vortex', and
later a collection of 'fields'). Either way, the table in front
of me (or the object that I 'picture as' a table) is described
by 'mathematical formulas', as Husserl says. And this, he
points out, is what above all came into Western thinking
with the Galilean revolution: the idea of the 'external
world' as something whose true description, whose
description 'in itself', consists of mathematical formulas.

It is important to this way of thinking that certain
familiar properties of the table—its size and shape and
location—are 'real' properties, describable, for example, in
the language of Descartes' analytic geometry. Other
properties, however, the so-called 'secondary' properties, of
which *color* is a chief example, are *not* treated as real
properties in the same sense. No 'occurrent' (non-
dispositional) property of that swarm of molecules (or that
space-time region) recognized in mathematical physics can
be said to be what we all along called its *color*.

What about dispositional properties? It is often claimed
that color is simply a function of *reflectancy*, that is, of the
disposition of an object (or of the surface of an object) to
selectively absorb certain wavelengths of incident light and
reflect others. But this doesn't really do much for the
reality of colors. Not only has recent research shown that
this account is much too simple (because changes of
reflectancy across edges turn out to play an important role
in determining the colors we see), but reflectancy itself
does not have one uniform physical explanation. A red star
and a red apple and a reddish glass of colored water are
red for quite different physical reasons. In fact, there may
well be an infinite number of different physical conditions
which could result in the disposition to reflect (or emit)
red light and absorb light of other wavelengths. A

dispositional property whose underlying non-dispositional 'explanation' is so very non–uniform is simply incapable of being represented as a mathematical function of the dynamical variables. And these—the dynamical variables— are the parameters that this way of thinking treats as the 'characteristics' of 'external' objects.

Another problem[3] is that *hues* turn out to be much more subjective than we thought. In fact, any shade on the color chart in the green part of the spectrum will be classed as 'standard green' by some subject—even if it lies at the extreme 'yellow-green' end or the extreme 'blue-green' end.

In sum, no 'characteristic' recognized by this way of thinking—no 'well-behaved function of the dynamical variables'—corresponds to such a familiar property of objects as *red* or *green* . The idea that there is a property all red objects have in common—the same in all cases— and another property all green objects have in common— the same in all cases—is a kind of illusion, on the view we have come more and more to take for granted since the age of Descartes and Locke.

However, Locke and Descartes did give us a sophisticated substitute for our pre-scientific notion of color; a substitute that has, perhaps, come to seem mere 'post-scientific common sense' to most people. This substitute involves the idea of a sense datum (except that, in the seventeenth and eighteenth century vocabulary, sense data were referred to as 'ideas' or 'impressions'). The red sweater I see is not red in the way I thought it was (there is no 'physical magnitude' which is its redness), but it does have a disposition (a Power, in the seventeenth and eighteenth century idiom) to affect me in a certain way—to cause me to have sense data. And these, the sense data, do truly have a simple, uniform, non-dispositional sort of 'redness'.

This is the famous picture, the dualistic picture of the physical world and its primary qualities, on the one hand, and the mind and its sense data, on the other, that philosophers have been wrangling over since the time of

Galileo, as Husserl says. And it is Husserl's idea—as it was the idea of William James, who influenced Husserl—that this picture is disastrous.

But why should we regard it as disastrous? It was once shocking, to be sure, but as I have already said it is by now widely accepted as 'post-scientific common sense'. What is *really* wrong with this picture?

For one thing, *solidity* is in much the same boat as color. If objects do not have color as they 'naively' seem to, no more do they have solidity as they 'naively' seem to.[4] It is this that leads Sellars to say that such commonsense objects as ice cubes do not really exist at all. What *is* our conception of a typical commonsense object if not of something solid (or liquid) which exhibits certain colors? What there really are, in Sellars's scientific metaphysics, are objects of mathematical physics, on the one hand, and 'raw feels', on the other. This is precisely the picture I have just described as "disastrous"; it is the picture that denies precisely the common man's kind of realism, his realism about tables and chairs.

The reply to me (the reply a philosopher who accepts the post-Galilean picture will make) is obvious: 'You are just nostalgic for an older and simpler world. This picture works; our acceptance of it is an "inference to the best explanation". We cannot regard it as an objection to a view that it does not preserve everything that laymen once falsely believed.'

If it is an inference to the best explanation, it is a strange one, however. How does the familiar explanation of what happens when I 'see something red' go? The light strikes the object (say, a sweater), and is reflected to my eye. There is an image on the retina (Berkeley knew about images on the retina, and so did Descartes, even if the wave aspect of light was not well understood until much later). There are resultant nerve impulses (Descartes knew there was some kind of transmission along the nerves, even if he was wrong about its nature—and it is not clear we know its nature either, since there is again debate about the significance of chemical, as opposed to electrical, transmissions from neuron to neuron.) There are events in the brain, some of which we understand thanks to the work of Hubel and Wiesel, David Marr, and others. And then—this is the mysterious part—there is somehow a 'sense datum' or a 'raw feel'. *This* is an *explanation*?

An 'explanation' that involves connections of a kind we do not understand at all ("nomological danglers", Herbert Feigl called them[5]) and concerning which we have not even the sketch of a theory is an explanation through something more obscure than the phenomenon to be explained. As has been pointed out by thinkers as different from one another as William James, Husserl, and John Austin, every single part of the sense datum story is supposition—theory—and theory of a most peculiar kind. Yet the epistemological role 'sense data' are supposed to play by traditional philosophy required them to be what is 'given', to be *what we are absolutely sure of independently of scientific theory*. The kind of scientific realism we have inherited from the seventeenth century has not lost all its prestige even yet, but it has saddled us with a disastrous picture of the world. It is high time we looked for a different picture.

Intrinsic Properties: Dispositions

I want to suggest that the problem with the 'Objectivist' picture of the world (to use Husserl's term for this kind of scientific realism) lies deeper than the postulation of 'sense data'; sense data are, so to speak, the visible symptoms of a systemic disease, like the pock marks in the case of smallpox. The deep systemic root of the disease, I want to suggest, lies in the notion of an 'intrinsic' property, a property something has 'in itself', apart from any contribution made by language or the mind.

This notion, and the correlative notion of a property that is merely 'appearance', or merely something we 'project' onto the object, has proved extremely robust, judging by its appeal to different kinds of philosophers. In spite of their deep disagreements, all the strains of philosophy that accepted the seventeenth-century circle of problems—subjective idealists as well as dualists and materialists—accepted the distinction, even if they disagreed over its application. A subjective idealist would say that there are only sense data (or minds and sense data, in some versions), and that 'red' is an intrinsic property of these objects, while persistence (being there even when we don't look) is something we 'project'; a dualist or a materialist would say the 'external' objects have persistence as an intrinsic property, but red is, in their case, something we 'project'. But all of these philosophers *have* the distinction. Even Kant, who expresses serious doubts about it in the first Critique (to the point of saying that the notion of a "Ding an sich" *may* be "empty"), makes heavy use of it in the second Critique.

Putting aside the Berkeleyan view (that there aren't really any external objects at all) as an aberrant form of the seventeenth-century view, we may say that the remaining philosophers all accept the account of 'redness' and 'solidity' that I have been describing; these are not 'intrinsic properties' of the external things we ascribe them to, but rather (in the case of external things) dispositions to affect us in certain ways—to produce certain sense data in us, or, the materialist philosophers would say, to produce certain sorts of 'states' in our brains and nervous systems. The idea that these properties are 'in' the things themselves, as intrinsic properties, is a spontaneous 'projection'.

The Achilles' Heel of this story is the notion of a disposition. To indicate the problems that arise—they have preoccupied many first-rate philosophical minds, starting with Charles Peirce's—let me introduce a technical term (I shall not introduce much terminology in this lecture, I promise!). A disposition that something has to do something *no matter what*, I shall call a *strict disposition*. A disposition to do something under 'normal conditions', I shall call an *'other things being equal' disposition*. Perhaps it would be wise to give examples.

The disposition of bodies with non-zero rest mass to travel at sub-light speeds is a *strict* disposition; it is physically impossible for a body with non-zero rest mass to travel at the speed of light. Of course, the notion of a 'strict disposition' presupposes the notion of 'physical necessity', as this example illustrates, but this is a notion I am allowing the 'scientific realist', at least for the sake of argument. What of the disposition of sugar to dissolve in water?

This is not a strict disposition, since sugar which is placed in water which is already saturated with sugar (or even with other appropriate chemicals) will not dissolve. Is the disposition of sugar to dissolve in *chemically pure water*, then, a strict disposition?

This is also not a strict disposition; the first counterexample I shall mention comes from thermodynamics. Suppose I drop a sugar cube in water and the sugar cube dissolves. Consider sugar which is in water, but in such a way that while the situation is identical with the situation I just produced (the sugar is dissolved in the water) with respect to the position of each particle, and also with respect to the numerical value of the momentum of each particle, all the momentum vectors have the exactly opposite directions from the ones they now have. This is a famous example: what happens in the example is that the sugar, instead of staying dissolved, simply forms a sugar cube which spontaneously leaps out of the water! Since every normal state (every state in which sugar dissolves) can be paired with a state in which it 'undissolves', we see that there are infinitely many physically-possible conditions in which sugar 'undissolves' instead of staying in solution. Of course, these are all states in which entropy decreases; but that is not impossible, only extremely improbable!

Shall we say, then, that sugar has a strict disposition to dissolve unless the condition is one in which an entropy decrease takes place? No, because if sugar is put in water and there is immediately a flash freeze, the sugar will not dissolve if the freezing takes place fast enough. . . .

The fact is that what we can say is that under *normal* conditions sugar will dissolve if placed in water. And there is no reason to think that all the various abnormal conditions (including bizarre quantum mechanical states, bizarre local fluctuations in the space-time, etc.) under which sugar would not dissolve if placed in water could be summed up in a closed formula in the language of fundamental physics.

This is exactly the problem we previously observed in connection with redness and solidity! If the 'intrinsic' properties of 'external' things are the ones that we can represent by formulas in the language of fundamental physics, by 'suitable functions of the dynamical variables', then *solubility* is also not an 'intrinsic' property of any external thing. And, similarly, neither is any 'other things being equal' disposition. The Powers, to use the seventeenth-century language, have to be set over against, and carefully distinguished from, the properties the things have 'in themselves'.

Intrinsic Properties: Intentionality

Well, what of it? Why should we not say that dispositions (or at least 'other things being equal' dispositions, such as solubility) are also not 'in the things themselves' but rather something we 'project' onto those things? Philosophers who talk this way rarely if ever stop to say what *projection* itself is supposed to be. Where in the scheme does the ability of the mind to 'project' anything onto anything come in?

Projection is thinking of something as having properties it does not have, but that we can imagine (perhaps because something else we are acquainted with really does have them), without being conscious that this is what we are doing. It is thus a species of *thought*—thought about something. Does the familiar 'Objectivist' picture have anything to tell us about thought (or, as philosophers say, about 'intentionality', that is, about *aboutness*)?

Descartes certainly intended that it should. His view was that there are two fundamental substances—mind and matter—not one, and, correspondingly there should be two fundamental sciences: physics and psychology. But we have ceased to think of mind as a separate 'substance' at all. And a 'fundamental science' of psychology which explains the nature of thought (including how thoughts can be true or false, warranted or unwarranted, about something or not about something) never did come into existence, contrary to Descartes' hopes. So to explain the features of the commonsense world, including color, solidity, causality—I include causality because the commonsense notion of 'the cause' of something is a 'projection' if dispositions are 'projections'; it depends on the notion of 'normal conditions' in exactly the same way—in terms of a mental operation called 'projection' is to explain just about every feature of the commonsense world in terms of *thought*.

But wasn't that what idealists were accused of doing? This is the paradox that I pointed out at the beginning of this lecture. So far as the commonsense world is concerned (the world we experience ourselves as *living* in, which is why Husserl called it the *Lebenswelt*), the effect of what is called 'realism' in philosophy is to deny objective reality, to make it all simply *thought*. It is the philosophers who in one way or another stand in the Neo-Kantian tradition— James, Husserl, Wittgenstein—who claim that commonsense tables and chairs and sensations and electrons are *equally real*, and not the metaphysical realists.

Today, some metaphysical realists would say that we don't need a perfected science of psychology to account for thought and intentionality, because the problem is solved by some philosophical theory; while others claim that a perfected 'cognitive science' based on the 'computer model' will solve the problem for us in near or distant future. I

obviously do not have time to examine these suggestions
closely today, but I shall indicate briefly why I believe that
none of them will withstand close inspection.

Why Intentionality is so Intractable

The problem, in a nutshell, is that thought itself has
come to be treated more and more as a 'projection' by the
philosophy that traces its pedigree to the seventeenth
century. The reason is clear: we have not succeeded in
giving the theory that thought is just a primitive property
of a mysterious 'substance', mind, any content. As Kant
pointed out in the first Critique, we have no theory of this
substance or its powers and no prospect of having one. If
unlike the Kant of the first Critique (as I read the *Critique
of Pure Reason*), we insist on sticking to the fundamental
'Objectivist' assumptions, the only line we can then take is
that *mental phenomena must be highly derived physical
phenomena in some way,* as Diderot and Hobbes had
already proposed. By the 'fundamental Objectivist
assumptions', I mean (1) the assumption that there is a
clear distinction to be drawn between the properties things
have 'in themselves' and the properties which are
'projected by us' and (2) the assumption that the
fundamental science—in the singular, since only physics
has that status today—tells us what properties things have
'in themselves'. (Even if we were to assume, with Wilfrid
Sellars, that 'raw feels'—fundamental sensuous qualities of
experience—are not going to be reduced to physics, but are
in some way going to be added to fundamental science in
some future century, it would not affect the situation
much; Sellars does not anticipate that *intentionality* will
turn out to be something we have to add to physics in the
same way, but rather supposes that a theory of the 'use of
words' is all that is needed to account for it.)

Modern Objectivism has simply become Materialism.
And the central problem for Materialism is 'explaining the

emergence of mind'. But if 'explaining the emergence of mind' means solving Brentano's problem, that is, saying in *reductive* terms what 'thinking there are a lot of cats in the neighborhood' *is*, and what 'remembering where Paris is' *is*, etc., why should we now think *that*'s possible? If reducing color or solidity or solubility to fundamental physics has proved impossible, why should this vastly more ambitious reduction program prove tractable?

Starting in the late 1950s, I myself proposed a program in the philosophy of mind that has become widely known under the name 'Functionalism'. The claim of my 'Functionalism' was that thinking beings are *compositionally plastic*—that is, that there is no one physical state or event (i.e., no necessary and sufficient condition expressible by a finite formula in the language of first-order fundamental physics) for being even a *physically possible* (let alone 'logically possible' or 'metaphysically possible') occurrence of a thought with a given propositional content, or of a feeling of anger, or of a pain, etc. *A fortiori*, propositional attitudes, emotions, feelings, are not *identical* with brain states, or even with more broadly characterized physical states. When I advanced this claim, I pointed out that thinking of a being's mentality, affectivity, etc., as aspects of its *organization to function* allows one to recognize that all sorts of logically possible 'systems' or beings could be conscious, exhibit mentality and affect, etc., in exactly the same sense without having the same matter (without even consisting of 'matter' in the sense of elementary particles and electromagnetic fields at all). For beings of many different physical (and even 'non-physical') constitutions could have the same functional organization. The thing we want insight into is the nature of human (and animal) functional organization, not the nature of a mysterious 'substance', on the one hand, or merely additional physiological information on the other.

I also proposed a theory as to what our organization to function is, one I have now given up—this was the theory that our functional organization is that of a Turing

machine. I have given this up because I believe that there
are good arguments to show that mental states are not only
compositionally plastic but also *computationally plastic*.
What I mean by this is that physically possible creatures
who believe that there are a lot of cats in the
neighborhood, or whatever, may have an *indefinite number
of different 'programs'*. The hypothesis that there is a
necessary and sufficient condition for the presence of a
given belief in computational (or computational *cum*
physical) terms is unrealistic in just the way that the
theory that there is a necessary and sufficient condition for
the presence of a table in phenomenalistic terms is
unrealistic. Such a condition would have to be infinitely
long, and not constructed according to any effective rule,
or even according to a non-effective prescription that we
could state without using the very terms to be reduced. I
do not believe that even all *humans* who have the same
belief (in different cultures, or with different bodies of
knowledge and different conceptual resources) have in
common a physical *cum* computational feature which
could be 'identified with' that belief. The 'intentional level'
is simply not reducible to the 'computational level' any
more than it is to the 'physical level'.[6]

If this is right, then the Objectivist will have to conclude
that intentionality *too* must be a mere 'projection'. But how
can any philosopher think this suggestion has even the
semblance of making sense? As we saw, the very notion of
'projection' *presupposes* intentionality!

Strange to say, the idea that thought *is* a mere projection
is being defended by a number of philosophers in the
United States and England, in spite of its absurdity. The
strength of the 'Objectivist' tradition is so strong that some
philosophers will abandon the deepest intuitions we have
about ourselves-in-the-world, rather than ask (as Husserl
and Wittgenstein did) whether the whole picture is not a
mistake. Thus it is that in the closing decades of the
twentieth century we have intelligent philosophers[7]
claiming that intentionality itself is something we project
by taking a 'stance' to some parts of the world (as if 'taking

a stance' were not itself an intentional notion!), intelligent philosophers claiming that no one really has propositional attitudes (beliefs and desires), that 'belief' and 'desire' are just notions from a false theory called 'folk psychology', and intelligent philosophers claiming there is no such property as 'truth' and no such relation as reference, that 'is true'''is just a phrase we use to 'raise the level of language'. One of these—Richard Rorty—a thinker of great depth—sees that he is committed to rejecting the intuitions that underly every kind of realism[8] (and not just metaphysical realism), but most of these thinkers write as if they were *saving* realism (in its Materialist version) by abandoning intentionality! It's as if it were all right to say 'I don't deny that there is an external world; I just deny that we *think* about it'! Come to think of it, this is the way Foucault wrote, too. The line between relativism *à la française* and Analytic Philosophy seems to be thinner than anglophone philosophers think! Amusingly enough, the dust-jacket of one of the lattest attacks on 'folk psychology'[9] bears an enthusiastic blurb in which a reviewer explains the importance of the book inside the dust-jacket by saying that most people *believe* that there are such things as beliefs!

"The Trail of the Human Serpent is Over All"

If seventeenth-century Objectivism has led twentieth-century philosophy into a blind alley, the solution is neither to fall into extreme relativism, as French philosphy has been doing, nor to deny our commonsense realism. There *are* tables and chairs and ice cubes. There are also electrons and space-time regions and prime numbers and people who are a menace to world peace and moments of beauty and transcendence and many other things. My old-fashioned story of the Seducer and the Innocent Maiden was meant as a double warning; a warning against giving up commonsense realism and, simultaneously, a warning against supposing that the seventeenth-century talk of 'external world' and 'sense impressions', 'intrinsic properties', and 'projections', etc., was in any way a Rescuer of our commonsense realism. Realism with a capital 'R' is, sad to say, the foe, not the defender, of realism with a small 'r'.

If this is hard to see, it is because the task of overcoming the seventeenth-century world picture is only begun. I asked—as the title of this lecture—whether there is still anything to say, anything really new to say, about reality and truth. If "new" means 'absolutely unprecedented', I suspect the answer is 'no'. But if we allow that William James might have had something 'new' to say—something new to *us*, not just new to his own time—or, at least, might have had a program for philosophy that is, in part, the right program, even if it has not been properly worked out yet (and may never be completely 'worked out'); if we allow that Husserl and Wittgenstein and Austin may have shared something of the same program, even if they too, in their different ways, failed to state it properly; then there is still something new, something **unfinished and important** to say about reality and truth. And that is what I believe.

The key to working out the program of preserving commonsense realism while avoiding the absurdities and antinomies of metaphysical realism in all its familiar varieties (Brand X: Materialism; Brand Y: Subjective Idealism; Brand Z: Dualism. . . . . .) is something I have called *internal realism*. (I should have called it pragmatic realism!) Internal realism is, at bottom, just the insistence that realism is *not* incompatible with conceptual relativity. One can be *both* a realist *and* a conceptual relativist . Realism (with a small 'r') has already been introduced; as was said, it is a view that takes our familiar commonsense scheme, as well as our scientific and artistic and other schemes, at face value, without helping itself to the notion of the thing 'in itself'. But what is conceptual relativity?

Conceptual relativity sounds like 'relativism', but has none of the 'there is no truth to be found. . . "true" is just

a name for what a bunch of people can agree on'
implications of 'relativism'. A simple example will
illustrate what I mean. Consider 'a world with three
individuals' (Carnap often used examples like this when
we were doing inductive logic together in the early
nineteen-fifties), **x1**, **x2**, **x3**. How many *objects* are there in
this world?

Well, I *said* "consider a world with just three
individuals", didn't I? So mustn't there be three objects?
Can there be non-abstract entities which are not
'individuals'?

One possible answer is 'no'. We can identify 'individual',
'object', 'particular', etc., and find no absurdity in a world
with just three objects which are independent, unrelated
'logical atoms'. But there are perfectly good logical
doctrines which lead to different results.

Suppose, for example, that like some Polish logicians, I
believe that for every two particulars there is an object
which is their sum. (This is the basic assumption of
'mereology', the calculus of parts and wholes invented by
Lezniewski.) If I ignore, for the moment, the so-called 'null
object', then I will find that the world of 'three individuals'
(as Carnap might have had it, at least when he was doing
inductive logic) actually contains *seven* objects:

World 1	World 2
x1, x2, x3	x1, x2, x3, x1 + x2, x1 + x3, x2 + x3, x1 + x2 + x3
(A world à la Carnap)	('Same' world à la Polish logician)

Some Polish logicians would also say that there is a 'null
object' which they count as a part of every object. If we
accepted this suggestion, and added this individual (call it

O), then we would say that Carnap's world contains *eight* objects.

Now, the classic metaphysical realist way of dealing with such problems is well-known. It is to say that there is a single world (think of this as a piece of dough) which we can slice into pieces in different ways. But this 'cookie cutter' metaphor founders on the question, 'What are the "parts" of this dough?' If the answer is that O, $x1$, $x2$, $x3$, $x1 + x2$, $x1 + x3$, $x2 + x3$, $x1 + x2 + x3$ are all the different 'pieces', then we have not a *neutral* description, but rather a *partisan* description—just the description of the Warsaw logician! And it is no accident that metaphysical realism cannot really recognize the phenomenon of conceptual relativity—for that phenomenon turns on the fact that *the logical primitives themselves, and in particular the notions of object and existence, have a multitude of different uses rather than one absolute 'meaning'.*

An example which is historically important, if more complex than the one just given, is the ancient dispute about the ontological status of the Euclidean plane. Imagine a Euclidean plane. Think of the points in the plane. Are these *parts* of the plane, as Leibniz thought? Or are they 'mere limits', as Kant said?

If you say, in *this* case, that these are 'two ways of slicing the same dough', then you must admit that what is a *part* of space, in one version of the facts, is an abstract entity (say, a set of convergent spheres—although there is not, of course, a *unique* way of construing points as limits) in the other version. But then you will have conceded that which entities are 'abstract entities' and which are 'concrete objects', at least, is version-relative. Metaphysical realists to this day continue to argue about whether points (space-time points, nowadays, rather than points in the plane or in three-dimensional space) are individuals or properties, particulars or mere limits, etc. My view is that God himself, if he consented to answer the question, 'Do points really exist or are they mere limits?', would say 'I don't know'; not because His omniscience is limited, but because there is a limit to how far questions make sense.

One last point before I leave these examples: *given* a version, the question, 'How many objects are there?' has an answer, namely 'three' in the case of the first version ('Carnap's World') and 'seven' (or 'eight') in the case of the second version ('The Polish Logician's World'). Once we make clear how we are using 'object' (or 'exist'), the question 'How many objects exist?' has an answer that is not at all a matter of 'convention'. That is why I say that this sort of example does not support *radical* cultural relativism. Our concepts may be culturally relative, but it does not follow that the truth or falsity of everything we say using those concepts is simply 'decided' by the culture. But the idea that there is an Archimedean point, or a use of 'exist' inherent in the world itself, from which the question 'How many objects *really* exist?' makes sense, is an illusion.

If this is right, then it may be possible to see how it can be that what is in one sense the 'same' world (the two versions are deeply related) can be described as consisting of 'tables and chairs' (and these described as colored, possessing dispositional properties, etc.) in one version *and* as consisting of space-time regions, particles and fields, etc., in other versions. To require that all of these *must* be reducible to a single version is to make the mistake of supposing that 'Which are the real objects?' is a question that makes sense *independently of our choice of concepts*.

What I am saying is frankly programmatic. Let me close by briefly indicating where the program leads, and what I hope from it.

Many thinkers have argued that the traditional dichotomy between the world 'in itself' and the concepts we use to think and talk about it must be given up. To mention only the most recent examples, Davidson has argued that the distinction between 'scheme' and 'content' cannot be drawn; Goodman has argued that the distinction between 'world' and 'versions' is untenable; and Quine has defended 'ontological relativity'. Like the great pragmatists, these thinkers have urged us to reject the spectator point of view in metaphysics and epistemology. Quine has urged us to accept the existence of abstract entities on the ground that these are indispensible in mathematics,[10] and of microparticles and space-time points on the ground that these are indispensible in physics; and what better justification is there for accepting an ontology than its indispensibility in our scientific practice? he asks. Goodman has urged us to take seriously the metaphors that artists use to restructure our worlds, on the ground that these are an indispensible way of understanding our experience. Davidson has rejected the idea that talk of propositional attitudes is 'second class', on similar grounds. These thinkers have been somewhat hesitant to forthrightly extend the same approach to our moral images of ourselves and the world. Yet what can giving up the spectator view in philosophy mean if we don't extend the pragmatic approach to the most indispensible 'versions' of ourselves and our world that we possess? Like William James (and like my teacher Morton White[11]) I propose to do exactly that. In the remaining lectures, I shall illustrate the standpoint of pragmatic realism in ethics by taking a look at some of our moral images, and particularly at the ones that underlie the central democratic value of *equality*. Although reality and truth are old, and to superficial appearances 'dry', topics, I shall try to convince you in the course of these lectures that it is the persistence of obsolete assumptions about these 'dry' topics that sabotages philosophical discussion about all the 'exciting' topics, not to say the possibility of doing justice to the reality and mystery of our commonsense world.

Lecture II

REALISM AND
REASONABLENESS[1]

Some questions in philosophical logic are able to divide
philosophers into warring camps. Since the middle of the
twentieth century, this has been the case with the question
of the status of dispositional statements (and with the
closely related question of the status of counterfactual
conditionals). For some philosophers dispositions are
simply part of 'the furniture of the universe'; for others, the
use of a dispositional notion in a philosophical analysis is
a sign of 'low standards', of willingness to 'explain the
obscure by the still more obscure'; while for still others
(perhaps the silent majority) dispositional notions are
unavoidable in what we do but troubling to the conscience.
This is a relatively new state of affairs: the writers who
make up the canon of 'Modern Philosophy' (or at least of
seventeenth-century to mid-nineteenth-century philosophy)
all availed themselves of the notion of a Power (i.e., a
dispositional property) without any visible pangs of
conscience.

Perhaps this is not surprising, as it is only since the
appearance of mathematical logic that we have realized
how hard it is to give an interpretation of counterfactual
conditionals and of dispositional predicates in truth-
functional[2] terms. But, in a way, it should have been
realized a long time ago that the talk of Powers in 'modern'
philosophy was problematical, for such talk is a hang-over
from medieval philosophy, not something that belongs in
its own right to the new picture. The heart of the new
picture is the new conception of the 'external' world, the

conception of the external world as governed by *strict* laws of the form with which we are familiar from the work of Newton and his successors. It is this conception that motivates the division of properties into primary and secondary, or into intrinsic properties of the external things and powers to affect the mind of the observer. A world governed by a system of differential equations is one thing; a medieval (or an Aristotelian) world governed by Substantial Forms which manifest themselves as 'tendencies' rather than as exceptionless laws is something else. The Cartesian picture is confused. It exhibits both modern physicalist and medieval 'tendency-ist' forms of explanation in an unhappy coexistence. The new image of nature—the World Machine—ought to have no place for the classical 'tendencies'.

In the previous lecture this was argued with the aid of the example of the color predicate 'red'. Something is red if it has a certain tendency—the tendency to produce certain 'sense impressions' (according to the seventeenth and eighteenth century story), or a certain 'brain-state' (an alternative to the dualist story that goes back at least as far as Diderot if not to Hobbes), or (in a story which is overly simple but at least avoids the mind-body problem) if it has the tendency to selectively absorb and reflect certain wavelengths of light. But what does 'have the tendency' mean? Tendencies, as I said in yesterday's lecture, do not exemplify the operation of strict laws (in the modern sense of 'strict law'); they are sloppy things, that manifest themselves 'under normal conditions'. To analyze the dispositional idiom we need an analysis of the phrase 'under normal conditions', or something similar, and, in fact, the attempts to produce a theory which have been made by contemporary authors[3] involve such notions as the 'similarity' of a whole possible world with another whole world—notions which attempt to express, or at least to substitute for, the desired notion of a 'normal' state of affairs. But the currently most fashionable of these—the notion of 'similarity' of possible worlds—only illustrates the distance of counterfactual (and dispositional) talk from the world picture of physics—illustrates it by introducing a metaphysical primitive which sticks out like a sore thumb.

Other philosophers content themselves with introducing dispositional predicates one by one, as needed, without any attempt to analyze or account for the general dispositional idiom. Sometimes this can be justified (from an 'Objectivist' point of view) by showing that the predicate so introduced is coextensive with a non-dispositional (perhaps a structural) predicate. But most dispositional notions—e.g., 'red', 'poisonous', 'tending to say *da* if the linguist says *gavagai* and both of them are watching a rabbit'— are almost certain not to be coextensive with predicates definable in the language of fundamental physics.

Certain other philosophers have suggested that dispositional predicates are not, in general, the sorts of predicates for which one ought to expect there to be necessary and sufficient conditions. Perhaps such a word as 'poisonous' is only partly defined; perhaps when we encounter a new substance that human beings are capable of ingesting or breathing or touching we just extend the notion of being poisonous as we extend our other notions (including the notion of what is 'normal') in the given circumstances.[4] Other philosophers have suggested that such dispositional statements as 'X is poisonous' do not predicate a *property* at all; they are ways in which we perform the speech act of *licensing an inference*. As the late J. L. Mackie put it, such statements can be assertible under appropriate conditions without possessing any property a realist would recognize as 'truth'. (They are 'not simply true', he claimed.[5]) What many of these theories have in common is a denial that the semantics of dispositional sentences is the classical bivalent truth-conditional semantics. Either dispositional sentences aren't 'simply true' and 'simply false' at all, these authors say, or else they are true and false only in certain cases (the cases in which the dispositional predicate has been defined), and remain to be given a truth value in all other cases. (On either form of the view, the dispositional predicate lacks a well-defined extension.)

As I mentioned in the last lecture, similar issues arise in connection with the notions of *causality* and of *explanation* (conceived of as a relation between events or between 'situations', rather than as a relation between statements). Like dispositions, causal and explanatory relations may be strict (the event or 'situation' described as the cause may be connected by strict laws with the event or situation which is taken to be the effect) or may be loose (the event or situation described as the cause may bring about the effect only 'under suitable circumstances'). And the loose causal relations are, once again, an embarrassment from the point of view of the 'Objectivist' picture—the picture of nature as the World Machine.

If we could define in physicalistic terms what it is for a feature of a situation to be only an 'attendant circumstance', we might be able to explain 'X brought about Y' as meaning that *given the attendant circumstances*, it followed from physical laws that Y would happen if X did; but unfortunately, an intrinsic distinction between situations which are capable of being 'bringers about' and situations which are only attendant 'circumstances' has much more to do with medieval (and Aristotelian) notions of 'efficient causation' than with post-Newtonian ones. And once again, some philosophers have proposed either to *reject* the loose causal and explanatory relations altogether[6], while others have proposed that the loose causal and explanatory relations[7] have only 'assertibility conditions' and not 'truth conditions'.

My own view—the view I began to sketch out for you in the last lecture—differs from all of these. These authors all assume we can make the distinction between what is 'simply true' and what has only 'assertibility conditions', or the cut between what is already true or false and what is an 'extension of previous use' (albeit one that we all make the same way), or between what is a 'projection' and what is an independent and unitary property of things in themselves. I think that, epistemically at least, the attempt to draw this distinction, to make this cut, has been a total failure. The time has come to try the methodological hypothesis that no such cut can be made.

I recall a conversation with Noam Chomsky many years ago in which he suggested that philosophers often take perfectly sensible continua and get in trouble by trying to convert them into dichotomies. Consider, for example, the continuum between the relatively 'subjective' (or, at least, interest- and culture-relative) and the relatively 'objective' (or, at least, interest- and culture-independent). Prephilosophically, most of us would probably agree on the ordering of the following properties along this continuum:

(1) Being very amusing (as in 'the behavior of young babies is often very amusing')

(2) Being a region of space which contains at least one hydrogen atom (assume classical physics for this one—no relativity or quantum mechanics, please!)

(3) Being soluble.

(4) A single case counterfactual conditional—e.g., the property we predicate of a particular match at a particular time when we say it *would have* lit *if* it *had been* struck at that time.

(5) Meaning 'Do you speak French?' (predicated of a particular utterance).

I suppose the average person might rank these predications as follows (taking the left hand end of the line to represent the 'subjective' and the right hand end to represent the 'objective'):

Being Amusing	**Counter-factual**	**Meaning '...........'**	**Being Soluble**	**Contains Hydrogen**

(A Plausible Objective-Subjective Ranking)

—Yet as soon as we are asked to make a 'Dedekind cut'—to turn this ranking into a dichotomy— we find that there is no agreement at all in our philosophical intuitions. Quine, for example would put the cut between 5 and 3— counting both dispositional predicates (such as 'soluble') and non-dispositional predicates from fundamental physics as 'objective' and all the others as more or less subjective (or 'second class', in his terminology). Some philosophers might disagree with me on the position of the meaning-assigment 5—some counting it as more 'objective' than the assignment of *solubility* to a substance—and draw the line after 1, 4, and 3. Philosophers who are 'comfortable' with counterfactuals would make still another choice for the location of the 'cut', placing it immediately after 1—i.e., counting 'amusing' as subjective and all the rest as 'objective'. But my own view, as I have said (and perhaps Chomsky's as well, if I understood him aright) is that the enterprise isn't worth the candle. The game is played out. We can make a rough sort of rank ordering (although even here there are disagreements), but the idea of a 'point at which' subjectivity ceases and Objectivity-with-a-capital-O begins has proved chimerical.

If this is right, then a number of other famous dichotomies must be abandoned. Two of these have already been mentioned, namely:

Projection/Property of the thing in itself

and

'Power'/ Property of the thing in itself

The rejection of these three dichotomies is the essence of the 'internal realism' I defended before this very assembly nine years ago.

My rejection of these dichotomies will trouble many, and it should. Without the constraint of trying to 'save the appearances', philosophy becomes a game in which anyone can—and, as a rule does—say just about *anything*. Unless we take our intuitions seriously, we cannot do *hard* philosophy at all. So I respect philosophers who insist that the traditional dichotomies are deeply intuitive, and who 'need a lot of convincing' before they will give them up.

But if philosophy which simply scorns our intuitions is not worth the candle, philosophy which tries to preserve *all* of them becomes a vain attempt to have the past over again. There are phenomena which really do challenge our intuitions—the phenomenon Husserl described in *Crisis of the European Sciences*, the breakdown of the great seventeenth-century project of trying to turn physics into metaphysics ('Objectivism')—the breakdown I described in the preceding lecture—is one such. On the one hand, seventeenth-century science succeeded in smashing the medieval foundations of knowledge—and not just of knowledge, but of religion, politics, and morality as well. On the other hand, the line of thinking that said, 'Well, if science smashed all that, well and good. Science will give us better in its place,' now looks tired. (It already seemed tired to Kant—and not because Kant was a foe of science or Enlightenment; on the contrary, he was a great scientist and a great man of the Enlightenment.) Science is wonderful at destroying metaphysical answers, but incapable of providing substitute ones. Science takes away foundations without providing a replacement. Whether we want to be there or not, science has put us in the position of having to live without foundations. It was shocking when Nietzsche said this, but today it is commonplace; *our* historical position—and no end to it is in sight—is that of having to philosophize without 'foundations'.

The impossibility of imagining what credible 'foundations' might look like is one phenomenon, but not the only phenomenon, that challenges our 'intuitions'. Since the end of the nineteenth century science itself has begun to take on a 'non-classical'—that is, a non-seventeenth-century-appearance. In the last lecture I described the phenomenon of conceptual relativity—one which has simple illustrations, like the ones I used, but which has become pervasive in contemporary science. That there are ways of describing what are (in some way) the 'same facts' which are (in some way) 'equivalent' but also (in some way) 'incompatible' is a strikingly non-classical phenomenon. Yet contemporary logicians and meaning theorists generally philosophize as if it did not exist. If claiming to abandon *all* our 'intuitions' is mere show, retaining all of them would require us to philosophize as if the phenomena I just reminded you of did not exist. The task of the philosopher, as I see it, is to see *which* of our intuitions we can responsibly retain and which we must jettison in a period of enormous and unprecedented intellectual, as well as material, change.

If I reject the dichotomies I depicted, it is not, then, because I fail to recognize their intuitive appeal, or because that intuitive appeal counts for nothing in my eyes. It is rather because these dichotomies have become distorting lenses which prevent us from seeing real phenomena—the phenomena I have been describing—in their full extent and significance.

Yet I still term myself a 'realist'—even if I spell it all in lower case—and *can* one be any sort of a realist without the dichotomies? In particular, is not the dichotomy between what is a 'human projection'—what is not 'simply true', what has 'assertibility conditions' rather than 'realist truth conditions'—and what is in the things 'in themselves' *constitutive* of realism?

Part of my answer to that question was given in the first lecture. Far from being constitutive of *commonsense* realism, that dichotomy tends to undermine it, as I tried to show. But another part of the answer must consist in showing that the rejection of this dichotomy is not a simple capitulation to garden-variety cultural relativism, or to the idea that every conceptual scheme is as good as every other.

What is strange about the fear that only the Metaphysical Realist can save fair Common Sense from Demon Relativism is that even Metaphysical Realists recognize that the writ of rationality runs farther than what they are pleased to call 'realist truth'. Mackie did not think that ordinary-language causal statements, e.g., 'the failure of the safety valve caused the boiler to explode', are 'simply true', but he would certainly have distinguished between 'reasonable' and 'unreasonable' ones. Perhaps such statements have only 'assertibility' conditions rather than 'truth' conditions, perhaps they are used to issue 'inference licenses' rather than to 'describe', but that does not make them arbitrary. If we license one another to expect X to dissolve when put in water when X is a piece of sugar, this is part of a practice whose success we can explain; and if we issued the same license when X was a piece of steel, nature would show us our mistake. In the same way, Quine denies that 'X means *Do you speak French?*' states a 'fact', even when X is the familiar French utterance, *Parlez-vous français?*; but he would certainly answer the question 'What does *Parlez-vous français?* mean?' with 'It means *Do you speak French?*' and not with 'It means *Coachman, stop, the road is jerky; look out! you will lose the turkey.*' That one answer to this sort of question has 'heuristic' value and the other does not is something he himself points out. (I am not claiming that Quine is a 'metaphysical realist', in my sense, since he does not accept the correspondence theory of truth; but his 'robust realism' has an important feature in common with metaphysical realism—namely, the existence of a sharp line between what there is a 'fact of the matter' about, and what has only 'heuristic' value, or value when our interests are less than 'theoretical'.)

In sum, my own position involves the denial of yet another dichotomy:

(Type of Statement)

Possesses only assertibility-conditions	VS.	Possesses truth-conditions

We can know that it is 'true', speaking with the vulgar, that the water would have boiled if I had turned on the stove, without having the slightest idea whether this 'truth' is 'realist truth' (Mackie's 'simply true') or only an idealization of 'warranted assertibility'. Nor need we suppose the question makes sense. Rejecting the dichotomy *within* kinds of 'truth'—kinds of truth in the commonsense world—is not the same thing as saying 'anything goes'.

Reality without the Dichotomies

How can one assure oneself that this is not sheer linguistic idealism? Perhaps the best place to start is with the explanation of internal realism that I gave in the first lecture. That explanation certainly sounds like 'linguistic idealism'; according to me, how many objects there are in the world (and even whether certain objects—individual space-time points, in the second of the examples I used— exist at all as individual 'particulars') is relative to the choice of a conceptual scheme. How can one propound this sort of relativistic doctrine and still claim to believe that there is anything to the idea of 'externality', anything to the idea that there is something 'out there' independent of language and the mind?

Well, it really isn't so hard. Look again at the picture I showed you:

World 1	World 2
x1, x2, x3	x1, x2, x3, x1+x2, x1+x3, x2+x3, x1+x2+x3
(A world à la Carnap)	('Same' world à la Polish logician)

How we go about answering the question, 'How many objects are there?'—the method of 'counting', or the notion

of what constitutes an 'object'—depends on our choice
(call this a 'convention'); but the *answer* does not thereby
become a matter of convention. If I choose Carnap's
language, I must say there are three objects because *that is
how many there are.* If I choose the Polish logician's
language (this is the language of a Polish logician who has
not yet invented the 'null object' **O**, remember), I must say
there are seven objects, *because that is how many objects*
(in the Polish logician's sense of 'object') *there are.* There
are 'external facts', and we can *say what they are.* What we
cannot say—because it makes no sense—is what the facts
are *independent of all conceptual choices.*

A metaphor which is often employed to express this is
the metaphor of the 'cookie cutter'. The things independent
of all conceptual choices are the dough; our conceptual
contribution is the shape of the cookie cutter.
Unfortunately, this metaphor is of no real assistance in
understanding the phenomenon of conceptual relativity.
Take it seriously, and you are at once forced to answer the
question, 'What are the various parts of the dough?'. If you
answer, that (in the present case) the 'atoms' of the dough
are **x1,x2,x3** and the other parts are the mereological sums
containing more than one 'atom', then you have simply
adopted the Polish Logician's version. Insisting that this is
the correct view of the metaphysical situation is just
another way of insisting that mereological sums *really*
exist. But internal realism denies that this is *more* the
'right' way to view the situation than is insisting that only
Carnap's 'individuals' really exist. The metaphysician who
takes the latter view can also explain the success of the
Polish Logician's Version, after all: he can say that when
the Polish Logician says, as it might be, that

**(I) There is at least one object which is partly red and partly
black.**

—this is to be understood as a useful *façon de parler*,
rather than as something which is 'literally true'. Under an
adequate translation scheme (and such a scheme can be
easily given in a recursive way, in the case of the kind of

first-order language that Carnap had in mind in these simple examples), **I** turns out to say no more than

(II) There is at least one red object and there is at least one black object.

—says when written in the Carnapian language. (To verify this, assuming that 'red' and 'black' are predicates of Carnap's language, observe that the only way a Polish Logician's object—a mereological sum—can be partly red is by containing a red atom, and the only way it can be partly black is by containing a black atom. So if **I** is true in the Polish Logician's language, then there is at least one red atom and at least one black atom—which is what **II** says in Carnap's language. Conversely, if there is at least one black atom and at least one red atom, then their mereological sum is an 'object'—in the Polish Logician's sense—which is partly red and partly black.) To claim that such a translation scheme shows what is 'really going on' is just a way of insisting that mereological sums *don't* 'really exist'.

The Cookie Cutter Metaphor *denies* (rather than explaining) the phenomenon of conceptual relativity. The other way of dealing with our little example—producing a translation scheme which *reinterprets the logical connectives (in this case, existence)*, in such a way that each statement in the 'richer' language can be 'translated' into the more 'parsimonious' language—may also be used to deny the phenomenon of conceptual relativity; but it is, nonetheless, more sophisticated than the Cookie Cutter Metaphor. The Cookie Cutter Metaphor assumes that all existence statements that we count as true in our several versions really are true; it's just that the variables of quantification pick out different mereological sums as their ranges in the case of different languages. The device of *reinterpretation* goes beyond this in recognizing that one person's 'existence' claim may be another person's something else.

Sometimes it is suggested that in such cases we should *not* be 'neutrals'; we should always adopt the more parsimonious version. 'If we don't have to postulate such strange discontinuous objects as mereological sums, then should't we take that as a reason for concluding that they don't really exist, that they are just (at best) a *façon de parler*?'

To this metaphysical move there is, inevitably, an equally metaphysical rejoinder: 'Aren't almost all the "objects" we talk about—chairs and tables, our own bodies, countries, not to mention such scientific objects as solar systems and galaxies—"strange discontinuous objects"? It hardly follows that they don't really exist. Yet, if my body exists, if this chair exists, if the solar system exists, then why should we not say that the discontinuous object consisting of *my nose and the Eiffel Tower* also exists? This is an unnatural object to talk about, to be sure, but what has the "naturalness" of an object to do with its *existence*?'

What is right with the second of the ways we considered of reconciling the two versions or 'worlds'—reinterpreting the existential quantifier—is that the notions of 'object' and 'existence' are not treated as sacrosanct, as having just one possible use. It is very important to recognize that the existential quantifier itself can be used in different ways— ways consonant with the rules of formal logic. What would be wrong, were we to do it, would be to accept this idea, and then go on to single out *one* use of the existential quantifier—the use in Carnap's Version—as the only metaphysically *serious* one. But go one step farther: take the position that one may *either* treat Carnap's Version as 'correct' and interpret the Polish Logician's Version as a *façon de parler* in the manner illustrated by the reinterpretation of **I** as **II**, or treat the Polish Logician's Version as 'correct' and interpret Carnap's Version as a language in which the range of the individual variables is restricted to atoms (as suggested by the Cookie Cutter Metaphor). That is, take the position that one will be equally 'right' in either case. Then you have arrived at the position I have called 'internal realism'!

What is wrong with the notion of objects existing 'independently' of conceptual schemes is that there are no standards for the use of even the logical notions apart from conceptual choices. What the Cookie Cutter Metaphor tries to preserve is the naive idea that at least one Category—the ancient category of Object or Substance—has an absolute interpretation. The alternative to this idea is not the view that, in some inconceivable way, it's all *just* language. We can and should insist that some facts are there to be discovered and not legislated by us. But this is something to be said when one has adopted a way of speaking, a language, a 'conceptual scheme'. To talk of 'facts' without specifying the language to be used is to talk of nothing; the word 'fact' no more has its use fixed by Reality Itself than does the word 'exist' or the word 'object'.

Of course, the adoption of internal realism is the renunciation of the notion of the 'thing in itself'. And here lies the connection between the almost trivial example we have been discussing and the profound metaphysical dichotomies (or would-be dichotomies) we discussed earlier. Internal realism says that the notion of a 'thing in itself' makes no sense; and *not* because 'we cannot know the things in themselves'. This was Kant's reason, but Kant, although admitting that the notion of a thing in itself *might* be 'empty', still allowed it to possess a formal kind of sense. Internal realism says that we don't know what we are talking about when we talk about 'things in themselves'. And that means that the dichotomy between 'intrinsic' properties and properties which are not instrinsic also collapses—collapses because the 'intrinsic' properties were supposed to be just the properties things have 'in themselves'. The thing in itself and the property the thing has 'in itself' belong to the same circle of ideas, and it is time to admit that what the circle encloses is worthless territory.

A dichotomy whose relation to these notions may be somewhat less evident is the dichotomy between 'truth conditional semantics' and 'assertibility conditional semantics'. Yet what could ground the claim that certain sorts of statements, for example, 'If I *had* put a pan of water on the stove and turned on the flame, the water *would have* boiled', have only 'assertibility conditions' and not 'truth conditions'? What, that is, but a preconceived idea of what is and is not 'ontologically queer', that is, what is and is not capable of being a part of the world as the world is 'in itself'? As I argued in yesterday's lecture, the problem with that preconceived idea, in its Humean as well as in its Cartesian version, was its inability to tell any story about the mind (or, if you prefer, about 'intentionality') which was not riddled with contradictions or saddled with arbitrary and unconvincing posits; and I argued that this remains its problem today.

What does the world look like without the dichotomies? It looks both familiar and different. It looks familiar, insofar as we no longer try to divide up mundane reality into a 'scientific image' and a 'manifest image' (or our evolving doctrine into a 'first-class' and a 'second-class' conceptual system). Tables and chairs (and yes, pink ice cubes) exist just as much as quarks and gravitational fields, and the fact that this pot of water would have boiled if I had put it on the stove and turned on the flame is as much a 'fact' as is the circumstance that the water weighs more than eight ounces. The idea that most of mundane reality is illusion (an idea which has haunted Western philosophy since Plato, in spite of Aristotle's valiant counterattack) is given up once and for all. But mundane reality looks different, in that we are forced to acknowledge that many of our familiar descriptions reflect our interests and choices.

Imagine that the escape valve on a pressure cooker sticks and the pressure cooker explodes. We say—and the conceptual relativist regards this as a perfectly 'true' statement, without making any fuss about whether it is 'simply true' or only a 'good inference license'—'The stuck valve caused the pressure cooker to explode'. We do not say 'The presence of Δ caused the pressure cooker to explode', where Δ is, say, an arbitrary irregularly shaped piece of the surface of the cooker, 0.1 cm. in area. Yet, in the physics of the explosion, the role played by the stuck valve is exactly the same as the role of Δ: the absence of either would have permitted the steam to escape, bringing down the pressure and averting the explosion.

Why, then, do we speak of one of these things and not the other as 'causing' the explosion? Well, we know that the valve 'should have' let the steam escape—that is its 'function', what it was designed to do. On the other hand, the surface element Δ was not doing anything 'wrong' in preventing the steam from escaping; containing the steam is the 'function' of the surface of which Δ is a part. So when we ask 'Why did the explosion take place?', knowing what we know and having the interests we do have, our 'explanation space' consists of the alternatives:

(1) Explosion taking place
(2) Everything functioning as it should

What we want to know, in other words, is why **1** is what happened, *as opposed to* **2**. We are simply not interested in why **1** is what happened *as opposed to* such alternatives as:

(3) The surface element Δ is missing, and no explosion takes place.

This 'explanatory relativity' is parallelled by a relativity in our use of such locutions as 'caused' and 'the cause'. Since the question 'Why did the pressure cooker explode?' assumes an explanation space which does not include the alternative **3**, or similar alternatives, we understand such factors as the presence of Δ to be 'background conditions' and not 'causes'.

This relativity of causes to interests, and to background conditions not mentioned in the 'hard science' explanation of the event in question, does not make causation something we simply legislate. Given our interests and what we regard as the relevant background conditions, it would be simply false to say that it was the wall of the pressure cooker that caused the explosion (unless it happened to be defective, and it should happen to be the defect and not the condition of the valve that 'explains' the explosion). Our conceptual scheme restricts the 'space' of descriptions available to us; but it does not predetermine the answers to our questions.

It is understandable, however, that many philosophers should read a different moral into this story. Does not the situation lend itself naturally to a dichotomy? Should we not regard the 'hard science' description of the situation ('The pressure increased in the closed container until a certain coefficient was exceeded. The material then ruptured...') with its exact laws and numerical coefficients as the description of the 'objective facts', and regard the singling out of the bit of material, or whatever, that kept the valve from working as 'the cause' as semi-magical Stone Age thinking? If we want to be generous and leave a place for this useful way of speaking, while denying that there exists a distinction between 'causes' and 'background conditions' in Nature Itself, we can just say that causal statements have 'assertibility' conditions in ordinary language but not, strictly speaking, 'truth conditions'.

The problem with all this—the problem I discussed in the first lecture—is that if the causes/background conditions distinction is fundamentally subjective, not descriptive of the world in itself, then current philosophical explanations of the metaphysical nature of *reference* are bankrupt. Barwise and Perry, for example, tell us that what links certain states of affairs to certain mental states is that the states of affairs *cause* those states; this is the intentional link, at least in certain metaphysically basic cases. Glymour and Devitt (independently) both tell us that words are connected to their referents by 'causal connection'. Richard Boyd tells us that 'the causal theory of reference is correct because the causal theory of knowledge is correct.' But the notions on which causal theories of knowledge and reference depend—the difference between a cause and a mere background condition, the legitimacy of counterfactuals— are precisely what is called into question by the 'inference licence' interpretation of causal statements and counterfactuals. If these notions are 'saved' only to the extent of being treated as heuristics (as 'projections', in the terminology of the first lecture), then it cannot also be held that they explain how reference comes to exist in the world as the world is 'in itself'.

Nor would dualism help, if we were willing to adopt it. For what description do we have of the mind 'in itself'? Kant's exposure of the bankruptcy of 'rational psychology' still stands.

Rather than succumb to the temptation to repeat verbatim all the proposals of the seventeenth and eighteenth centuries, we have to recognize that such familiar statements as the statement that the stuck valve caused the pressure cooker to explode reflect both the way things are and our interests and assumptions about the way things are *without* giving in to the temptation to suppose that the philosophically relevant description of 'the way things are' is something *other* than 'the valve stuck and caused the pressure cooker to explode' (or whatever the example may be). *Given* a language, we can describe the 'facts' that make the sentences of that language true and false in a 'trivial' way—using the sentences of that very language; but the dream of finding a well-defined Universal Relation between a (supposed) totality of *all* facts and an arbitrary true sentence in an arbitrary language, is just the dream of an absolute notion of a fact (or of an 'object') and of an absolute relation between sentences and the facts (or the objects) 'in themselves'; the very dream whose hopelessness I hoped to expose with the aid of my little example involving three Carnapian individuals and seven non-empty mereological sums.

Lecture III

EQUALITY AND OUR MORAL IMAGE OF THE WORLD

In the preceding lecture, I tried to explain and defend a position that combines elements of 'realism' with elements of 'antirealism'. Many have perceived that my position belongs to the Kantian tradition (broadly conceived). And it may be well to say something about the relationship between my views and the work of Kant.

There are readings of Kant on which such a relationship is not at all apparent, just as there are some readings of Kant on which the relationship of what I am about to say to Kant's moral philosophy will not be at all apparent. And the fault is not entirely on the part of Kant's readers. Kant has, in a way, two philosophies. Kant says in places that the notion of a *Ding an sich*, a 'thing in itself', may be empty—an interpretation of this in contemporary language (a controversial one, to be sure) might be to say that while thoughts about what things are like 'in themselves' may be syntactically well formed, and while it may be that we have a natural propensity to engage in such thoughts, they lack any real intelligibility. I think that almost all of the *Critique of Pure Reason* is compatible with a reading in which one is not at all committed to a Noumenal World, or even, as I said, to the intelligibility of thoughts about noumena.

Kant gave very strong arguments for the view just described, the view that we cannot really form any intelligible notion of a noumenal thing. Yet, when Kant came to write his moral philosophy, he postulated a 'need of pure practical reason' which requires us to believe that

the idea of 'noumena' makes *some* kind of sense, even if
we are unable to say what kind of sense that is, and in the
service of which we must posit certain particular things
about the noumenal world: that we are noumenally free;
that after death we will somehow approach the *Summum
Bonum*; and that there is some noumenal Reality that
deserves the name 'God' (although Kant cautiously says
that God may not be a person, that this may only be the
way we have to think of Him in this life). In this picture—
the picture we must accept in order to satisfy the 'needs of
practical reason'—there are two worlds. In one world, the
'world of experience', all of the points made by Kant when
he takes the position I first described are valid, and
scientific knowledge—which is the only *knowledge* that is
properly so called, according to Kant—cannot go beyond
this world. In the other world, the world behind the veil,
there is God, Freedom, and Immortality. But obviously,
there can't be *only* God, Freedom, and Immortality.

I am repelled, as many philosophers have been repelled,
by this dualism of a noumenal and a phenomenal world.[1]
But this is not—repeat, *not* — Kant's only philosophy. It
seems to me that the real thrust of the *Critique of Pure
Reason* is quite different. What led Kant into keeping a
double set of books was not, I think, his conception of
truth, but his mistaken ideas about moral philosophy,
specifically the mistaken idea that moral philosophy is
impossible without transcendental guarantees that can be
given only if we posit a noumenal realm.

If Kant's *Critique of Practical Reason* fails, in these
respects, as morality, it seems to me that it also fails as
religion. For the religious person, the place of God in
morality should not be primarily to dole out rewards and
punishments, as it is (sometimes) in Kant's scheme. Nor is
it any service to religion to think of God as an object
behind a veil—a veil so thick that the very conceivability
of anything behind it must be in doubt. But our relation to
the divine is not the subject of these lectures. My subject is
rather the clue provided by the reading of the *first* Critique,
in which Kant's philosophy is not committed to, but rather

suggests a rejection of, the distinction between things in themselves and projections. On such a reading the 'things for us' of the first Critique are simply *things*, not 'projections', and the point of the first Critique *isn't* that all we know is 'experiences' in the Empiricist sense, that is, that all we know is sense data. The first Critique as I would read it, *rejects* the notion of a sense datum, that is, of an object whose 'essence is to be perceived' and in whose constitution the conceptual system plays no role. Sensations for Kant—the 'objects of inner sense'—are on a level with so called 'external objects'. They are as much caught within the web of belief and conceptualization as are external objects. They do not represent an uncorrupted 'given', that somehow *anchors* our knowledge. I will not go into further details because this is not a historical lecture. I will only remind you that in *Reason, Truth and History* I presented Kant as the first philosopher to reject the idea of truth as correspondence to a pre-structured Reality.

If Kant *was* saying that truth must not be thought of as correspondence to a pre-structured or self-structured Reality; if he was saying that our conceptual contribution cannot be factored out and that the 'makers-true' and the 'makers-verified' of our beliefs lie *within* and not *outside* our conceptual system; then Kant may properly be called the first 'internal realist'. It is true that he does not endorse the sort of conceptual relativity I advocated in my first lecture. On the contrary, he thinks that we have exactly one *scientific* version of the world. Yet, I wonder whether there is not a *hint* of conceptual relativity in the fact that in each Critique—not just in the first two—we are presented with a different *kind* of reason, and with what might be called a different image of the world to go with each kind of reason: scientific reason, ethical reason, aesthetic reason, juridical reason. But again this is not a historical lecture. I am claiming Kant as a forefather, not treating him as Scripture.

I have just criticized Kant's moral philosophy, for it is there if anywhere that we find the double set of books, the idea of a world behind a veil and a world for us, as in the stock image of 'Kantianism'. Yet I want to say that even in the second Critique there is a deep tension. The second Critique more than any other defends the image to which I object. Yet, I shall claim, it presents ideas that can be separated from that image, ideas that may be the beginning of a kind of 'internal realism' in moral philosophy. It is those ideas, and, more broadly, the idea of 'internal realism' in moral philosophy, that I want to sketch in the remaining lectures of this series.

I want to suggest that Kant's moral philosophy represents, above all, a rethinking of the values that Kant took from Rousseau (and of the fundamental ideals of the French revolution), in particular of the value of Equality. The value of Equality is, perhaps, a unique contribution of the Jewish religion to the culture of the West. Greek ethics, as we know it in Plato and in Aristotle and even in the Hellenistic period, has no notion of universal human equality. The idea of equality appears in the Jewish Bible as the idea that all human beings are created in the image of God. This is connected with some features of the Jewish legal code, for example, the fact that the life of one Israelite is worth as much as the life of any other Israelite, the eye of one Israelite is worth as much as the eye of any other Israelite, and so on. What makes this point of view a radical innovation when compared to the Code of Hammurabi and to other ancient codes, is that these latter applied the idea of 'equal penalties' only to social equals: a nobleman who killed a slave only had to pay a money fine. The idea of a set of penalties that should ignore social class, the idea of a justice which in the Biblical idiom does not 'respect persons', that is, show partiality, was a concretization of equality.

Later, of course, the idea of equality was detached from its specifically religious roots; one effect of this separation, an effect we see right to the present day, is that the idea of equality becomes somewhat *mysterious*, and, for that reason, exposed to scoffing. I sometimes wonder how many people really do believe any longer in human equality, or

only say that they do out of a certain sentimentality.
Perhaps the following two principles, vague as they are,
may capture the minimal content that the idea of equality
which Western culture took from the Bible seems to have:

**(I) There is something about human beings, some aspect
which is of incomparable moral significance, with respect
to which all human beings are equal, no matter how
unequal they may be in talents, achievements, social
contribution, etc.**

**(II) Even those who are least talented, or whose
achievements are the least, or whose contribution to
society is the least, are deserving of respect.**[2]

These principles say that we should show one another a
mutual respect that treats as irrelevant differences in
talents and achievements. (The idea that we owe respect to
the untalented, and to those whose achievement is not
significant—he didn't care about 'social contribution'—is
one that Nietzsche attacked vehemently, and it is because I
regard it as fundamentally right that I do not fully share
the current admiration for Nietzsche.)

To these two principles a third seems to have been
added in the course of the centuries, as the notion of
'happiness' came to play an ever more central role in
ethical thinking. This is that:

**(III) Everyone's happiness or suffering is of equal prima
facie moral importance.**

All three of these principles can be and have been taken
over into totally secular moralities. For example, although
the Jerusalem-based religions take the respect of equality
(the "something about human beings") mentioned in **I** to
be 'being made in God's image', another possible choice,
especially as 'rights' talk comes to be more and more
uncritically used, is to say that the respect of equality is

simply that every human being has certain 'rights', and that
we are all equal with respect to these fundamental rights.
Or, in circles in which the notion of 'happiness' comes to
be central rather than the notion of 'rights', one may say
that the third principle should be used to interpret the
first; that is to say, the equal importance of the happiness
of every person *is* precisely the respect with respect to
which persons are equal. And, as I said, there are moralists
who think that the whole idea is just a mistake; that there
is *no* aspect of any significance with respect to which all
human beings are equal; these moralists advocate various
forms of moral elitism and reject the moral tradition which
derives from the Jewish and Christian religions, as
Nietzsche did. One thing, however, is clear: in the
traditional formulations, theistic and secular alike, the
value of equality does not have much to do with
individual *freedom*. What I am going to suggest is that
Kant offered a radically new way of giving content to the
notion of equality, a way that builds liberty into equality.
John Rawls,[3] who also acknowledges Kant as a forerunner,
has produced an interpretation of 'Kantian constructivism'
which has an intimate relation to the reinterpretation of
Kant that I shall offer; in effect, I shall argue that Kant was
more 'Rawlsian' than appears on the surface.

How does Kant understand equality? In my
interpretation, the crucial point is the presence of a certain
kind of scepticism in Kant's thinking, a scepticism about
what is most taken for granted in traditional moral theory
prior to Kant. I shall come to this in a moment. First let me
say this: everyone recognizes that Kant's central distinction
is the distinction between autonomy and heteronomy. But
what exactly *is* that distinction? The formula is easy to
recite: one is heteronomous if one is, for example, simply
browbeaten into accepting a moral system, or if one
accepts a moral system just because one's parents and
teachers believe it, or if one accepts a moral system
'unthinkingly', that is, if it never even occurs to one to
'think for oneself'. Kant is very fond of the maxim 'think
for yourself', which he regards as the great maxim of the

Enlightenment, and frequently repeats it both in German and in Latin. In Kant's point of view, what the Church tried to produce in the Middle Ages, what all churches have at times tried to produce, and what modern totalitarians try to produce, is heteronomous people.

It is clear enough what 'heteronomy' is like. It is not so clear what 'autonomy', or to use another of Kant's phrases, 'self-legislation', comes to. Of course, 'autonomy' is the contradictory of 'heteronomy'. But what we do want is a positive characterization. What is it to be an autonomous person or a self-legislating person in the moral sphere, exactly? It sounds like free choice, and Kant does believe in Free Will, but it certainly isn't a free choice in the sense of an arbitrary choice, an *acte gratuit*. Kant does think that there is a kind of reason possible in ethics, and that even if we cannot show by reason alone that the premisses of any ethical system are true, we can show that certain moral principles must be right *if* there is any objective morality at all. This is the famous transcendental approach to ethics, and this is where Kant himself sees the parallelism between the second Critique and the first; but this isn't going to be quite what I see as the parallelism.

The autonomous person asks 'Was soll ich tun?', what should I do?, how should I live?, and he uses his reason in trying to figure out the answer, even if he doesn't use it in quite the way the medievals, for example, thought he should use it. But so far, you see, it is hard to see how this really differs from the medieval picture. If an autonomous person is one who is conscious of having free will and reason, and who uses his free will and his reason in the choice of ethical principles, then is it so clear that he is doing anything different from what Thomas Aquinas would have had him do? Thomas gives a great deal of scope to the 'natural light', and recognizes the possibility of arriving at a good deal of ethics by the 'natural light'; thus he might agree with much of Kant, if all the vision of human beings as autonomous comes to is that human beings have free will and reason. We are, any medieval would say, rational beings with free choice; but the

Kantian notion of autonomy is not *just* the medieval notion of freedom plus rationality. It is only by seeing the specific difference between the two notions that we can appreciate the respects in which Kantian autonomy is a radical notion, and it is only by appreciating these that we can come to see the respects in which Kant provided a *deep* foundation for the notions of equality he received from the tradition and from Rousseau.

Not to keep you in suspense, the point is quite simple; according to the medievals, as Alasdair MacIntyre[4] has reminded us, we possess a capacity to know the human 'function' or the human 'essence'. We might also express their view by saying we know what Happiness (or Eudaemonia) is, where Happiness is understood in the 'thick' Aristotelian sense; that is, not just as a positive feeling, or a combination of gratifications, but as the 'inclusive human end'. If this medieval view is right, and we know what the human essence is, what the human *ergon* is, what the inclusive human end is, and we are capable of knowing all this by using reason, then the problem of using rationality and free will, first to discover what one should do and then to do it, is, in certain ways analogous to an engineering problem. The engineer has to solve his problem, perhaps with his computer (we can no longer say 'with pencil and paper'), perhaps with the aid of some laboratory tests, and then he has to apply the solution. So we have to figure out what we are required to do given the human function, given the nature of Eudaemonia, perhaps to lead the contemplative life, or perhaps to live lives of civic virtue, etc.—these are, of course, not the same ideal; one is Greek and the other is Roman—or to be good Christians or Jews or Moslems, or whatever, and then, having determined this, we have to do it. And we can be given good or bad marks both for our success or failure to figure out what the objective standard requires of us and for our success or failure in living up to it. But (*pace* Alasdair MacIntyre) Kant understands that this will no longer wash. In the *Grundlegung*[5] he says explicitly that one cannot build an ethic upon the notion of Happiness, because too many different things can be made out to be the content of that notion. This Kantian *scepticism* is what I want to call to your attention.

If Kant is right, our position is not at all the one Thomas Aquinas took us to be in. To be blunt, we are called upon to use reason and free will in a situation which is in certain important respects very dark. The situation is dark because reason does not give us such a thing as an inclusive human end which we should all seek (unless it be morality itself, and this is not an end that can determine the *content* of morality). Kant's move, or one of Kant's moves—for I think that here too there is a tension in Kant's thought, and there is certainly a side in Kant that goes back to something very close to the medieval picture—but in the strain in Kant that I am explicating, the idea is to take this very situation and, instead of regretting it or bemoaning it, to say that it is exactly what we should desire! To say that it would, in fact, be bad if there were a revealed human *ergon* or revealed nature of Eudaemonia.

Why would it be bad? It would be bad because we shouldn't *want* to be heteronomous, and the medieval picture is one that forces on us a certain kind of heteronomy. To me the most revealing passage in perhaps all of Kant's moral writing, the passage in which he most reveals how the idea of this kind of objective inclusive human end repulses him, is in the post-critical essay titled 'Religion within the Bounds of Reason alone'. In this essay Kant makes the remarkable statement (many would say it is an absurd statement) that it would be a bad thing if the truths of religion could be deduced by reason, because that would produce fanaticism.

Notice how Kant is using the term 'fanaticism'. He is saying—and with deep psychological insight—that what makes the fanatic a fanatic isn't that his beliefs are necessarily wrong or his arguments incorrect. It is possible to have true beliefs supported by correct arguments, and still to be what Kant calls a 'fanatic'; it is possible to have the kind of undesirable intolerance, intensity, in short, hostility to others thinking for themselves, that represented 'fanaticism' to the Enlightenment, and still be perfectly logical. In fact the perfecty logical fanatic, Kant is saying, is the most dangerous kind of fanatic. Fanaticism, Kant is saying, is undesirable in itself. That the truths of religion— which for Kant are the most important truths—should be by their very nature *problematic* is a good thing, not a bad one. This is where Kant's break with the medievals is total.

At the same time, Kant is not advocating *fideism*. In the same essay he attacks the idea of basing religion on pure 'faith' as *also* leading to 'fanaticism'. Kant tells us, in effect: 'Let us recognize that we have a religious need, but let us not be fanatical about the way in which we satisfy that need.' He thinks that we can satisfy ourselves of the *genuineness* and *legitimacy* of the religious need by reason; but he does not regret—on the contrary, he celebrates—the fact that reason cannot tell us how to satisfy that need, and he does not think that we should make a 'leap of faith' into Fundamentalism of some kind in order to satisfy it, either. This leaves him (and us) with a problem, of course: where do we get any *content* for religion, if neither reason nor blind faith can provide it? Kant's own answer is that the only content on which we are justified in relying is our right to *hope*; understanding the legitimacy of that hope is still a use of reason; but any hypostatization of the particular conception of the divine that a particular 'church' may have into an absolute goes beyond the limits of reason and invites fanaticism (or, as we would say today, 'Khomeiniism'). In this respect, Kant's attitude is the same as Lessing's. "There is one religion and many churches", Kant writes somewhere.

As I said, I find these remarks about rationalism and fideism in theology terribly revealing. What Kant is saying, to put it positively, is that we have to think for ourselves without the kind of guide that Alasdair MacIntyre wants to restore for us, and that fact is itself the most valuable fact about our lives. *That* is the characteristic with respect to which we are all equals. We all are in the same predicament, and we all have the potential of thinking for ourselves with respect to the question of How to Live.

If I read him aright, Kant's ideal community is a community of beings who think for themselves without knowing what the 'human essence' is, without knowing what 'Edaemonia' is, and who respect one another for doing that. *That* is Kant's 'Kingdom of Ends'.[6]

Notice, by the way, how far Kant is from Rousseau's notion of submission to the *volunté general* (and this even though Kant enormously admired Rousseau—Rousseau's picture was the only picture in Kant's study, and it has been claimed[7] that Kant's whole project derives from Rousseau). Whereas the minimum notion of equality that I described before can be reconciled with various sorts of totalitarianism, Kant's notion cannot. Freedom of thought is essential, because the fundamental characteristic with respect to which we are equal, our so to speak 'respect of equality', is precisely our need for, our capacity for, free moral thinking.

My claim then, is that Kant is doing what he would have called 'philosophical anthropogy', or providing what one might call a *moral image of the world*.[8] He is not simply providing arguments for the third formulation of the Categorical Imperative, arguments for the proper ordering of the formal and material principles of morality, and so on; he is also, and most importantly, providing a moral image of the world which *inspires* these, and without which they don't make sense. A moral image, in the sense in which I am using the term, is not a declaration that this or that is a virtue, or that this or that is what one ought to do; it is rather a picture of how our virtues and ideals hang together with one another and of what they have to do with the position we are in. It may be as vague as the notions of 'sisterhood and brotherhood'; indeed, millions of human beings have found in those metaphors moral images that could organize their moral lives—and this notwithstanding the enormous problem of interpreting them and of deciding what it could possibly mean to make them *effective*.

Now, moral philosophers generally prefer to talk about virtues, or about (specific) duties, rights, and so on, rather than about moral images of the world. There are obvious reasons for this; nevertheless, I think that it is a mistake, and that Kant is profoundly right. What we require in moral philosophy is, first and foremost, a moral image of the world, or rather—since, here again, I am more of a pluralist than Kant—a number of complementary moral images of the world.

But first, it is easy to see a similarity between this side of Kant and the strain I like in Kant's epistemology. For the medievals, metaphysical realism was unproblematically correct, because we were supposed to have a special faculty, the faculty of 'rational intuition', which gives us direct access to the things in themselves, or at least to their 'forms'. The negative or sceptical aspect of the first Critique lies in Kant's insistence that we don't have this kind of 'rational intuition'. Although Kant does recognize a number of kinds of intuition, for example, the so-called 'pure intuition' of the geometer, he denies that we have the medieval 'rational intuition'. Kant's glory, in my eyes, is to say that the very fact that we cannot separate our own conceptual contribution from what is 'objectively there' is not a disaster. It is, in fact, a certain kind of guarantee; at least as the thought is reconstructed in contemporary terms by Strawson,[9] what is sound in Kant's argument is that the notion of a future (or of a space-time) about which we are *wholly* mistaken is an incoherent one. If there is something we can call a 'future' at all, it must turn out that a great many of our beliefs about it are, in fact, true. I don't wish to say that this is as great a comfort as Kant thought it was (nor does Peter Strawson wish to claim this), but it is an important point, nonetheless, that many kinds of scepticism turn out, on close examination, to be incoherent. Similarly, I am suggesting, Kant rejects the idea that we have something analogous to the medieval 'rational intuition' with respect to moral questions. And again he argues that this is no disaster, that on the contrary it is a Good Thing. The whole Kantian strategy, on this reading, at least, is to *celebrate* the loss of essences, without turning back to Humean empiricism.

The Frankfurt School's Attempt to Justify Equality

There is another attempt to explain and justify the value of equality which derives inspiration from the work of Kant, however, and it is fitting that I should mention it here; I am thinking of the work of Jürgen Habermas[10] and Karl-Otto Apel.[11] This work is too complex to discuss in detail, but the leading ideas are well-known. Habermas and Apel claim—and I agree—that the notion of a warranted or justified statement involves an implicit reference to a community. They moreover believe that engaging in discourse which lays claim to rationality implicitly commits one to certain claims: to claims as to the truth, sincerity, justification, etc., of what one says, for example. They explain that the idea of a fully *justified* statement is the idea of a statement that can withstand tests and withstand criticism. (This is a 'tenseless' or absolutized notion of a justified statement, not the notion of a statement which is 'justified on present evidence', or 'justified for someone in such-and-such a position'.) Even when we make a statement which cannot ordinarily be subject to real doubt, for example, 'I am raising my hand', one can think of far-fetched cases in which the statement can successfully be called into question. There was the famous occasion on which G. E. Moore gave as an example of a certainty, 'I know there is a window in this room' and on which Moore was, in fact, mistaken (Moore was lecturing in a hall at the University of Michigan which has curtains, but no windows behind the curtains). The idea of a statement whose complete and final warrant is wholly available to the speaker himself *no matter what happens*— or of a speaker who neither needs nor can benefit from the data of others—is precisely the old notion of knowledge which is private and incorrigible. The interesting thought is that if Peirce and Wittgenstein are right (and Apel refers a good deal to both Peirce and Wittgenstein), and private knowledge and incorrigible knowledge are empty and fallacious ideas, then there can be no such thing as a statement which is true (or, at any rate, a statement which is true humanly speaking, i.e., capable of withstanding all possible attempts to falsify it) unless there is the possibility of a community of testers or, at any rate, critics.

The upshot is that *if I am a rational person in the sense of having the aim of making statements which are true humanly speaking, i.e., which can withstand rational criticism now and in the future, then I am committed to the idea of a possible* community *of inquirers.* (In fact, to the idea of a possible community of potentially infinite size, since there can be no such thing as a final inquirer if every inquiry is allowed to be reopened.)

So far this may not seem to have anything to do with ethics, although it has a lot to do with Pragmatist conceptions of reasonableness. But what *sort* of community must this ideal community be? If I say something aiming at truth and at warrant, then I am, according to Apel and Habermas, *recognizing the authority* (at least in principle) *of an ongoing community, a community which must have a certain structure.* A community which is competent to determine truth and falsity must be such that, for example, anyone in that community can *criticize* what is put forward knowing that his criticism will be attended to; if some criticisms are simply not heard, then the possibility of an irrational sort of 'protection of belief' rears its ugly head; we are back at what Peirce called the Method of Authority. Again, not only must it be possible for any member of the community to ask a question or voice a criticism, it must also be possible for any member of a community of ideal inquirers to advance a hypothesis knowing that it will be heard. It must, in short, be a community which respects the principles of intellectual freedom and equality.

Still, one may say that it is possible to recognize the value of having communities which obey an ethic of equality and intellectual freedom, while at the same time not believing that those principles should be universalized. One may keep slaves, as the ancient Greeks did, while at the same time discussing with great intellectual freedom with one's fellow slaveowners whether slavery is or is not justified. But, as Habermas has insisted, there is something, after all, to the Marxian notion of 'false consciousness'; Aristotle's inquiry into the ethics of slavery was not really 'free'; the conclusion was a foregone one.

Again, one might claim that the need for communities of inquirers which respect the principles of equality and intellectual freedom does not really imply that tyrannical societies are in any way 'irrational'. A tyrant could after all, want to have a community of scientists, and he could even allow them a certain freedom of speech, as long as they restricted their free speech to the laboratory. But the tyrant will not feel that this commits him to the value of free speech in civil society. Apel and Habermas would reply by pointing out that he is not going to allow the scientists free speech on social and political questions, and to that extent he is not allowing them *full* freedom of inquiry. If the tyrant claims his own political beliefs are *rational* while protecting them from rational criticism, then he is involved in a kind of contradiction.

I have said enough to indicate why I think that the position of Apel and Habermas is an extremely interesting one, and worthy of more attention from analytic philosophers than it currently receives. But the conclusion I would draw from what I think are the very real insights of Apel and Habermas is not that one can derive a universal ethic from the idea of reasonableness, or from the (Kantian as well as Peircian) picture of truth as idealized rational acceptability, but a different, weaker but still important conclusion. Habermas is right: there is a real tension between wishing one's beliefs to be completely rational and tolerating a society which restricts intellectual freedom in fundamental ways. There is a further tension involved in claiming to have a society that does not at all restrict intellectual freedom while justifying any form of oppression.

A problem with attempting to derive a universal ethic from these considerations, however, is that one's opponent may *not* claim that his ethical beliefs are rational. Indeed, if he is a 'non-cognitivist', he may deny that *any* ethical beliefs are or could be rationally justified. This in itself might not bother a philosopher arguing in the Kantian tradition, since such a philosopher may (like Kant himself) be content to show that certain values are rationally justified *if* there are any rationally justified values at all. But a second problem arises when one is arguing with an opponent who is an elitist: the opponent may insist that democratically structured societies *themselves* produce 'false consciousness'. The fact that a certain measure of egalitarianism and intellectual freedom is necessary in a community of physical scientists does not show that it is necessary or desirable in a community whose aim is to achieve the Superman, he may say; a Nietzschean will insist that it is only in a certain kind of *inegalitarian* society that the truth about human existence can shine through.

These objections do not show that Apel's and Habermas's attempts to derive the values of equality and intellectual freedom from rationality are without value. Their arguments *do* show that our values of equality, intellectual freedom, and rationality, are deeply interconnected. But the moral that I would draw from this is more Aristotelian than Kantian: we have a rich and multifaceted idea of the good, and the parts of this idea are interdependent.

Although, as I have said, internal realism does have a familial connection to Kantianism, the way in which I shall diverge the most from Kant is in not trying (or even pretending to try) to derive ethics from reason alone. That project was part of the eighteenth-century dream of a 'universal ethics'—a dream that was not always separated, as Sidney Morgenbesser has remarked in conversation, from the dream of a 'universal way of life'. While the relation of the reasonable and the ethical is part of my story, my belief is that there is another part of the story that we must attend to—another part which, paradoxically, also comes from Kant.

Democracy without a Moral Image

One way to see the importance of a Philosophical Anthropology, of a moral image of the world, is to see what results when we try to justify our fundamental social institutions—especially the institution called 'democracy'—without appealing to an image of human nature. Perhaps the most common defense of democracy is Winston Churchill's. I am speaking of the famous wisecrack, 'Democracy is the worst of all systems—except, of course, for all the others that have actually been tried.' Winston Churchill was giving a real argument for democracy—everything else we know works *worse*. But this defense, though it is strong and important, would be vulnerable should a real Technocracy come into existence with means for conditioning its citizens to accept its values (and to feel 'happy'). Recently I happened to read Huxley's profound novel *Brave New World* for the first time. I found it a philosophically very important book. So I tried to discuss it with my friends, who had all read it. Unfortunately, it turned out that they had all read it in high school or even in junior high, and 'didn't remember it very well'. So I still haven't been able to discuss it with anyone who remembers reading it and reacting to it as an adult. It is a great pity that this book has been relegated to the high school years (where it can be presented as a criticism of 'them'—the totalitarians—and not as a criticism of *us*), because the dialogue near the end of the book with Mustafa Mond, the World Controller, while not, perhaps, as great a piece of literature as the famous dialogue with the Grand Inquisitor, is a beautifully achieved fictional contemplation of deep issues. You will recall (I hope) that in *Brave New World* people are, in a sense, 'happy'. They certainly enjoy a high 'hedonic tone', and have an enormous amount of 'fun'. Without cheating, it is hard to see how classical pleasure-based Utilitarianism could deny that, if they haven't actually *maximized*

'Happiness', they have certainly achieved a lot more happiness in *that* sense than did the society that Huxley's Distopia replaced. The argument that democracy works better than the alternatives we know works fine as long as the alternatives we know lead to wars and to poverty and to gross suffering; but Huxley's Distopia has abolished war, abolished all the obvious forms of suffering, and so on. The price, in the novel, is a deliberate *infantilization* of the human race. People are conditioned to remain emotionally adolescent for their whole lives, and to enjoy adolescent pleasures for as long as they live, and only adolescent pleasures. If its citizens could be taken to the present day, and allowed to see our present democratic society with its stresses and strains, its emotional conflicts, its political conflicts, and so on, the premiss of the novel is that the great majority of them would want to flee back to their infantile pleasures (and to their drug 'soma').

I have said that classical Utilitarianism does not really have a non-cheating answer to the question, 'What's wrong with Huxley's Brave New World?' (assuming the premisses of the novel). It may be thought that modern Utilitarianism does, however. Modern Utilitarianism (I shall call it 'Preference-Function Utilitarianism') is based on the idea of giving people what they *prefer* (hence the frequent references to the economists' notion of a 'preference function'). What is wrong with Huxley's Dystopia, a modern Preference-Function Utilitarian might say, is that people (that is, people *now*) would not *prefer* to live in the Brave New World, and the Preference-Function Utilitarian insists that Happiness is to be determined by people's preference functions *as they are now*—not as they would be after suitable conditioning. But what Huxley's novel brings out is a point that is often missed in these discussions. What is missed is that Preference-Function Utilitarianism is simply a way of 'smuggling into' Utilitarianism a value other than Happiness; namely, the value of *free choice*, without bringing into the picture any of the resources for defending that value that could come from a 'thick' image of human nature.

What I have in mind is this: if Bernard, in his dialogue with the World Controller, had said that the society is bad because it is not the society that the people in the preceding age would have chosen if they had had a free choice (remember that the age immediately preceding was an age of chemical warfare and biological warfare on the scale of a holocaust), Mustafa Mond would simply have laughed. After all, it is the 'best society' according to the preference functions of the people who live in it, even if those preference functions are the product of conditioning. That conditioning is strong to be sure, but it is not the whole story. The infantile pleasures they enjoy, drugs and sex and 'thrills' and so on, are real pleasures, the sufferings that come with emotional commitment, with loyalties and friendships, with political and religious commitments, and so on, are real sufferings. These people *as they are* in *their* world genuinely prefer their world. It is the world that 'maximizes happiness' by the standard provided by the preference-functions they actually have. Why should we make a fetish out of satisfying the preference functions people have without conditioning, as opposed to making them happy even if making them happy requires *changing* those preference functions? Mustafa Mond argues that controlled experiments have been tried, experiments using the most intelligent part of the population and giving them the chance to form a free society. Those experiments resulted once again, he tells us, in war and destruction. The point is that Mustafa Mond *has* an image of the world, even if we find it a repulsive one—a naturalistic and reductionist image—and he has a strong case that, in the lights of his image, it is clear that his society makes people *happy*.

I said a moment ago that Preference-Function Utilitarianism is really a way of smuggling a second value into Utilitarianism. My hypothetical dialogue between a Preference-Function Utilitarian and Mustafa Mond (which is not too far from the actual dialogue in the book) was designed to make this clear. In effect, the Preference-Function Utilitarian is insisting that we must make people

happy, but we must do this without impairing their
freedom to decide for themselves what their Happiness *is*.
This is not one value ('Happiness') but two; in fact, it is
three, for a principle that I listed before in my description
of the 'minimal Jerusalem-based notion of equality',
namely, the principle that *everyone's happiness (or lack of
it) is of equal prima facie importance*, is assumed by all
forms of Utilitarianism.[12] Utilitarianism is an attempt to
make a series of ideas which have deep and complex roots
in our culture, values of equality, liberal values of choice,
and values of fraternity and happiness, seem simple and
non-arbitrary. As I said before, the more one tries to do this
without examining those values severally, and examining
the images of the world that can support those values, the
worse off one is going to be; for if all those values rest on
is an unexamined general notion that 'people ought to be
happy', then, as I say, the challenge of Mustafa Mond, the
challenge of one who says, 'Why on earth should one who
is thinking *scientifically* about happiness assume that
every Tom, Dick, and Harry is a good judge of his own
happiness?' will rapidly become unanswerable. I don't
know, in fact, which is more terrifying: the Distopia
described by Huxley, who describes it with distaste, or the
Utopia described by Skinner in *Walden Two*, who
describes it with positive relish.

The point I want to make is that the defense of liberal
values, especially the defense of intellectual freedom, with
which Kant was so concerned, cannot be entrusted to
Utilitarianism if the only way the Utilitarian can defend
them is by smuggling them into his definition of
'happiness' in what is, after all, an intellectually
undefended way. Utilitarianism is an inadequate vision for
just the reasons Kant gave: the uselessness of the notion of
'happiness', and the insensitivity of happiness-based ethics
to issues about *means*.

Kant's is not, of course, the only alternative moral image
we have. The Jerusalem-based religions had an image
which, while it did not yet include the liberal values of
free and critical thinking, stressed equality and also

fraternity, as in the metaphor of the whole human race as
One Family, of all women and men as sisters and brothers.
And I myself find Kant's moral philosophy defective in
two respects. Kant does not want to supplement earlier
moral images, but to replace them completely, and to
replace them with a monistic moral standpoint. We need a
more pluralistic vision than the eighteenth century could
foresee. I can also sympathise with those who think that
the replacement of a notion of fraternity which stresses the
idea of having fraternal *feelings* towards one another by a
notion of fraternity which stresses doing one's *duty*
towards one another involves a real loss. Thus I disagree
with Kant's rigorism *and* I think we need a more multifaceted moral image of the world. Not only do we have a
Jerusalem-based image based on Fraternity-one which
again becomes secularized, as 'Liberty, Equality, Fraternity'
becomes *the* great slogan of the French Revolution—we
have another image coming from Roman thought, but today
revived by some liberal and even left-wing thinkers, the
image of Roman 'civic republicanism', which stresses the
idea of *homo sapiens* as a creature who derives his dignity
and his identity from his membership in a *polis*, and
whose highest duty is not 'contemplation' but the exercise
of the civic virtues. We have many different moral images
in our tradition, and there are moral images which we
need to pay attention to in other traditions as well. But it
seems to me that a genuine morality must always reflect a
substantial moral image. Otherwise the image that Mustafa
Mond advances in *Brave New World*, or the image Skinner
advances in all seriousness in *Walden Two*—the image of
human happiness as a merely *technical* problem—will
always begin to assert its 'scientific validity'.

As I pointed out, to describe an ideal as a moral image is
to say that it is far more than a characterization of some
one trait or some one mode of behavior as virtuous. The
Kantian moral image does include the claim that thinking
for oneself about how to live (*für sich selbst denken!*) is a
virtue, to be sure, but it contains many other ideas as well.
It contains the idea that this virtue is not just a virtue, but

that our capacity for exercising this virtue is the most significant moral capacity we have; it includes the claim that a human being who has chosen not to think for himself about how to live, or has been coerced or 'conditioned' into being unable to think for himself about how to live, has failed to live a fully human life. It contains also the vision of a community of individuals who respect one another for that capacity, and ideas about how such a community should be organized and about the moral position that the members of such a community are in, about what they can and cannot know. In short, it is a vision which includes and organizes a complex system of values. The same thing is true of the system of beliefs that constitutes the tradition of civic republicanism that I mentioned a moment ago. And even the metaphor of the human 'family', of universal sisterhood and brotherhood, vague as it is, has served to organize moral thinking and to give a meaning to morality for a hundred generations of human beings.

If this is right, however, then our problem may seem harder, not easier. Individual 'values', duties, virtues, and so forth, are hard enough to justify; how on earth can one hope to justify a whole moral vision, a 'Philosophical Anthropology'? Both the complexity and the elasticity, or possibility of different interpretations, of the aims which are organized by any moral image is going to be a source of difficulty. But a discussion of *this* issue must be postponed to the next and final lecture.

Lecture IV

REASONABLENESS AS A FACT
AND AS A VALUE

At the present point, I would not be surprised if many of
my hearers felt inclined to say something like this: 'The
moral images you described in the last lecture are
splendid, wonderful, but look! Any serious philosopher
will ask how we can *justify* any of this.'

In a book I published some years ago,[1] I defended the
idea that something can be both a fact and a value—I said
that it is a fact, for example, that Yeats was a great poet,
and a fact that the Nazis were evil. And then too, it was
the question of justification that bothered people. Very
often people expressed their worry by asking: 'But don't
you have to admit that there is much more agreement on
scientific results than on ethical values? Doesn't that show
that there is a kind of objectivity that scientific results have
and that ethical values lack?'

An argument is implicit in the question. We might call it
the *argument from non-controversiality*. The idea is that
the hallmark of cognitive status is, in some way, the
possibility of becoming 'public' knowledge, i.e., of
becoming non-controversial.

I don't mean to suggest that anyone really thinks that
only what is non-controversial is really knowledge. The
idea, rather, is that 'facts' can be demonstrated
'scientifically'. If there is controversy over a factual
question, that is because we have not yet performed
enough experiments, or amassed enough data. What is a
fact can 'in principle' be established in a way that will
command the assent of all 'rational persons', where this is

often taken to mean all *educated* persons, or all *intelligent* persons. Thus Weber[2] argued that value judgements can only be a matter of 'faith'; and he thought this was sufficiently established by pointing out that there were some Western values of whose correctness he could not convince a "Chinese Mandarin". The issue I want to begin with today is this supposed 'public' character of fact, the idea that fact can 'in principle' be established beyond controversy.

It is not at all clear that this idea is correct even for the 'hard sciences'. Science has changed its mind in a startling way about the age of the universe, and it may do so again. If establishing something beyond controversy is establishing it *for all time*, as opposed to merely establishing it so that it is the accepted wisdom of one time, then it is far from clear how much fundamental science is, or ever will be, 'established beyond controversy'. The issue is familiar to philosophers of science from discussions of 'convergence', and I do not propose to pursue it here.

One reason that my interlocutor's question cannot be dismissed by pointing out how 'controversial' the issue of convergence in theoretical science is, is that the questioner is likely to say that there is convergence with respect to the *observational* results, at least. Here too there are problems, of course. At one time 'simultaneous' seemed to be an observation term (in such predictions as 'if you do X, the system will simultaneously Y and Z'). But since the acceptance of the Theory of Special Relativity, we are aware of a strong 'theoretical' component in the notion of simultaneity. A similar point could be made about other 'observational' terms.[3] But my interlocutor would not be putting this question to me if he believed Tom Kuhn's[4] story about the 'incommensurability' of even the observational vocabularies of the sciences. So he will just say that even if our *theory* of simultaneity, or whatever, has changed, still there is *something* invariant about the kind of prediction I have just mentioned.

Let me, rather, just *give* my interlocutor his idea that we get convergence, consensus, freedom from controversy, in the hard sciences, at least 'in principle'. The question which deserves a long hard look is: 'What follows?' Does the presence of disputes which cannot be settled in other areas, areas we do not count as 'real science', really show that 'subjective' or 'cognitively meaningless' statements are being made? And (since I have recently been teaching William James) What would be the consequences for our lives of *seriously* answering 'yes' to this question? What is the 'cash value' of believing that only what can be established beyond controversy has anything to do with 'cognition', knowledge, understanding?

It is not small. Consider, for a moment, our *historical* knowledge. I recently had occasion to read a work by a great historian[5] who built a powerful case for the view that 'medieval' civilization did not really begin with the fall of Rome. Under the Merovingian kings, this historian argued, the civilization which prevailed was still recognizably 'Roman'. The drastic changes which created what we still picture as 'medieval' civilization—the disappearance of Latin, except among very learned monastics, the ascendance of the North German princes, the complete break with Byzantium, the whole feudal order—came about as a consequence of the rise of Islam, and of the Islamic conquest of Egypt, Roman Africa, and Spain. This is a typical example of a historical reconstruction. We all know that such reconstructions are, as a rule, extremely controversial. Let us imagine that this particular reconstruction continues to be so. What are we to conclude?

If we take seriously the idea that controversiality indicates lack of 'cognitive' status, then we would be compelled to believe that this historian has made no 'cognitively meaningful' claim—a conclusion which seems absurd on the face of it!

My interlocutor might respond by saying that the principle that what is fact can be established beyond controversy is intended to apply only to fundamental existence claims. If the fundamental existence claims presupposed by an investigation or by a whole discipline have been verified 'publicly', then individual hypotheses formulated in terms of the entities and properties whose existence has been thus established do not need to be individually testable to count as cognitively meaningful. (The Logical Empiricists made such a move when they changed from 'testability' to 'expressibility in an empiricist language' as the 'criterion of cognitive significance'.)[6] The existence of the Middle Ages, of Merovingians, of Pippin and Charlemagne and the Pope and Byzantium, etc., are non-controversial, he might point out, and this justifies our regarding individual hypotheses about them as cognitively significant.

There are two problems (at least) with this response, however. First of all, the hypothesis in question is a hypothesis about the causes of a whole social framework, a hypothesis about 'what happened because,' or, alternatively, about what would not have happened if the rise of Islam had not happened. Has the existence of global causal explanations, or of facts about what would not have happened if a certain unrepeatable historical event had not happened, been itself 'scientifically' established? It is hard to see how. Indeed, there are philosophers who would regard all such statements as cognitively meaningless. Secondly, as I remarked in the first lecture, the list of objects whose 'real existence' has not been established by 'hard science' (according to leading philosophers) is impressive indeed—even ice cubes don't make it, according to Sellars! In fact, what science says about the *behavior* of ice cubes is far clearer than whether science says they 'really exist'.

A different response was offered long ago by Ernest Nagel[7] and also by Reichenbach[8] and other empiricists of his school. According to these philosophers, the inferences made by historians are simply inductive inferences of the same sort that we see in physics. If those inferences do not lead to very high degrees of confirmation (according to these thinkers), that is because social science is still 'immature'; we have not yet discovered the laws of social behavior. When we have succeeded in formulating these, then we will be able to determine in a more satisfactory way which of the presently available interpretations of social events are acceptable and which are not.

Today, however, the very belief that there *are* 'laws of social behavior' of an exact sort—and the belief that the fate of social science is to come to resemble physics—has become a minority view among social scientists and also among philosophers and methodologists of the social sciences. Certainly this is an empirical claim; if it is false, then historical theories such as the one I took as an example cannot be verified beyond significant controversy in this way.

Reichenbach would not, I think, have been as disturbed as Nagel was by this possibility. My memories of him from the time I was his student lead me to think that he might have said something like this, 'Sometimes we have to accept theories which are only weakly confirmed, when all the alternatives are even more improbable. The fact that historical theories do not attain a high degree of probability, and perhaps never will, does not mean that the nature of the inductions that we use to measure that probability is in any way special.'

If this view is right, then what is special about 'science' is not at all the possibility of establishing the truth of hypotheses more or less conclusively (beyond controversy). This view concedes one of the things it is my concern to argue for: that a hypothesis or a statement may be warranted, may be reasonable to believe, in an objective sense of the words 'warrant' and 'reasonable', even though we cannot specify an experiment (or data) such that were we to perform it (or were we to collect them) we would be able to confirm or disconfirm the hypothesis to an extent which would command the assent of all educated and unbiased people. According to Reichenbach's view,[9] what is essential about science is its use of 'induction', and not at all the possibility of getting the woman on the street (or the educated woman on the street) to believe its results.

My interlocutor might, of course, say that we could settle the controversy about the causes of the characteristic features of 'Medieval' civilization *by producing a large number of possible worlds just like our own prior to the birth of Mohammed, but in which Mohammed wasn't born, and seeing what happens*, but this would be science fiction rather than methodology. Or, he might say that 'some evidence may turn up which we cannot now envisage and which will decide the issue—we may even discover those laws of social science that Ernest Nagel hoped for.' But there is all the difference in the world between saying an issue is 'settlable in principle' in the sense that one can describe experiments—experiments humanly posssible to perform—whose outcome would confirm or disconfirm the hypothesis to a very high degree, and saying 'something may turn up'. There are, after all, thinkers[10] who hold that most ethical disagreement is an unrecognized by-product of factual disagreement: if people agreed on social and psychological theory, in the widest sense (conceptions of human nature, and society), then, these thinkers claim, they would come to agree on most disputed ethical issues. It is not logically impossible that this view is right; so 'in principle' something may turn up that will settle most ethical disagreement. This is not the question that the person who asks whether ethical disagreements could be settled is asking: he is asking whether we can *now* specify findings that would settle ethical controversies.

Sometimes, in fact, he is asking for something even stronger. Robert Nozick reports being asked whether one could give an argument to show that Hitler is a bad man *that would convince Hitler himself*. The only answer to this demand—the demand that what is fact must be provable to every 'intelligent' person—is to point out that probably no statement except the Principle of Contradiction—has this property.[11]

Finally, my interlocutor could just bite the bullet and deny that historical hypotheses (such as the one I mentioned) *do* have cognitive status. This is the most interesting move open to him, and there are at least some philosophers and social scientists who are tempted by it. But what would it mean to *seriously* believe such a thing?

The fact is that every cultured person does have an image of the Middle Ages, of the Roman Empire, of the Renaissance, etc. These images are not cast in concrete; since History reached maturity as an intellectual discipline in the nineteenth century, they have been repeatedly revised, and the work of cliometricians and social historians is leading to still further revisions at the present time. Still other innovations in historical method will lead to still other revisions in the future. But, even if my images of the past are not absolutely correct, I regard them as better than nothing. I take the attitude toward them that Reichenbach would have recommended. What would it mean to regard everything I believe about the past except the 'bare historical record' (*is there* such a thing?) as *fiction*?

Again, consider *political* opinions, insofar as they deal with 'factual' as opposed to 'moral' issues. Each of us has many views about 'what would happen if' this or that political, or foreign political, or economic, or social policy were implemented, and many views about 'what would have happened' if this or that policy *had not* been implemented. Even if some of our moral views do not depend on these beliefs, most of us are sensitive to consequences in deciding what policies our moral views entail; if one has no beliefs at all about which actions are most likely to avoid war, or to bring peace in the Middle East, or to make jobs, or to provide shelter for the homeless, then how could one have a political position at all? Yet these judgements too resist the kind of settlement that would put them beyond controversy. Even when we predict correctly what the result of a given policy will be, the morals we draw from the success of our prediction are usually hotly disputed. And it is easy to dispute them, for our claims about 'what would have happened' if *other* policies had been instituted instead (the ones advocated by our political opponents, in the case in which it was our policy that was carried out and the success we anticipated resulted; the ones we advocated, in case it was the opponent's policy that was carried out) are such complex counterfactual assertions that no way to 'prove' or 'disprove' them—no way to put them beyond controversy—exists. Again, one *could*, I suppose, take the view that all such views are no more than fictions: and a consequence might be the attitude that 'truth' in such matters is to be determined by imposing one's will; the true political philosophy is the one that succeeds in imposing itself, and in resisting attempts to overthrow it.

What is wrong with relativist views (apart from their horrifying irresponsibility) is that they do not at all correspond to how we think and to how we shall continue to think. I remember Donald Davidson's once asking me the rhetorical question: 'What is the point of saying that intentional idioms are 'second class'[12] if we are going to go on using them?' The question was a good pragmatist question. The heart of pragmatism, it seems to me—of James's and Dewey's pragmatism, if not of Peirce's—was the insistence on the supremacy of the agent point of view. If we find that we must take a certain point of view, use a certain 'conceptual system', when we are engaged in practical activity, in the widest sense of 'practical activity', then we must not simultaneously advance the claim that it is not really 'the way things are in themselves'. Although philosophers have traditionally allowed themselves to keep a double set of books in this way, the effect is to perpetuate at least two intellectualist errors: it leads one to debase the notion of *belief* (remember, Pragmatism was inspired by Bain's definition of belief—'of that upon which a man is prepared to act'); and it leads one to indulge in the fiction that there is a God's Eye point of view that we can usefully imagine. Our *lives* show that we believe that there are more and less warranted beliefs about political contingencies, about historical interpretations, etc.

Of course, my prediction that we will continue to talk this way, that we will continue to speak of political analyses and historical theories as more or less warranted, even if controversy continues to be permanent, may be falsified. We may come to think of history and politics as nothing but power struggle, with truth as the reward that goes to the victor's view. But then our culture—everything in our culture that is of value—will be at an end.

This is not, it may seem, an argument. It will be said that I have only pointed out that belief in this sort of scientism—in a scientism which *seriously* holds that everything that cannot be settled beyond controversy is non-cognitive—would have disastrous consequences, and that this does not show the view is false. I plead 'guilty'. In extenuation, let me say that I have argued elsewhere that Verificationist views (and the rhetorical question that my interlocutor asked was, I think, an expression of a pre-philosophical kind of Verificationism) are self refuting.[13] My purpose today was different. My purpose was to break the grip that a certain picture has on our thinking; the picture of a dualism, a dichotomous division of our thought into two realms, a realm of 'facts' which can be established beyond controversy, and a realm of 'values' where we are always in hopeless disagreement. What I hope to have reminded all of us of—and I include myself, for we all slip back into the picture at times—is the vast stretches of our thought that do not consist of 'value judgements', but which are, on the other hand, just as 'controversial' as value judgements. No sane person should believe that something is 'subjective' merely because it cannot be settled beyond controversy.

Scientific Method

The picture I have been discussing is, as I said, a pre-philosophical image rather than a sophisticated view. A more sophisticated way of defending the fact-value dichotomy is to argue, with Reichenbach,[14] that factual statements (*including* the controversial sorts of factual statements we have been discussing) can be confirmed or disconfirmed by the scientific method, while 'value judgements' cannot be. In *Reason, Truth and History*[15] I argued that this appeal to 'the scientific method' is empty. My own view, to be frank, is that there is no such thing as *the* scientific method. Case studies of particular theories in physics, biology, etc., have convinced me that no one paradigm can fit all of the various inquiries that go under the name of 'science'. But let me not presuppose any of this today. Let me assume, for the sake of argument that Reichenbach is right, or rather, that a view like Reichenbach's is right (since Reichenbach's own conception of the scientific method, that it can *all* be reduced to 'the straight rule of induction' is not acceptable today). Ethics, we will concede is not cognitive. On the other hand, we can still believe that historical theories and counterfactuals are cognitively meaningful, since (according to Reichenbach) these can be confirmed using 'the scientific method', even if the inferences are not as good as one might like (which is why they remain controversial). Let us see what the consequences might really be.

First of all, let us see what is problematical about the inferences used in history, if these are thought of simply as 'inductive inferences'. Let us consider an example simpler than the one I used before. In his autobiography, Collingwood includes a fascinating chapter about his own work on Roman Britain. The problem that he tried to solve is the reappearance of ancient Celtic styles in the decorative arts after Britain ceased to be a part of the Roman world. One explanation might be that the inhabitants had continued to produce such art *during* the Roman period, but all the evidence we have is against this. In fact, it seems that the Celtic *motifs* were regarded as barbaric and even as wicked during the Roman period. So Collingwood tries a psychological hypothesis: (according to this hypothesis) the very fact that these *motifs* were taboo made them objects of fascination. People kept describing them to their children (while explaining that they were very, very 'wicked'), and *this* is what kept the memory alive.

It is easy to see how Carnap or Reichenbach could regard this as a species of inductive inference. I shall not quarrel with anyone who wants to call it such. But notice: if it is an 'induction', it is an induction of the most problematical sort. For our evidence for the psychological generalization that *calling things 'wicked' causes a fascination to attach to them* comes from cases which are different from the Celtic-art-in-Roman-Britain case in every particular. What we are dealing with, in old fashioned terminology, is *induction by analogy* rather than the application of a precise (universal or statistical) law which has been scientifically tested.

When Carnap and I worked together on inductive logic in 1953-54, the problem that he regarded as the *most* intractable in the whole area of inductive logic was the problem of 'giving proper weight to analogy'. No criterion is known for distinguishing 'good' from 'bad' analogies, and a well-known argument of Nelson Goodman's[16] shows that a purely *formal* criterion is ruled out. Reichenbach himself admitted that he had no prescription for preventing contradictions from arising in inductive logic if one simply followed his formal procedure, and proposed to fix things up as one went along on an *ad hoc* basis, writing:[17] "With respect to the requirement of consistency, inductive logic differs intrinsically from deductive logic; it is consistent not *de facto*, but *de faciendo*, that is, not in its actual status, but in a form to be made." One recalls John Stuart Mill's remark (writing a hundred years before Reichenbach) that one cannot do science by slavishly following the rules of Mill's *Logic* (there is no general method, Mill remarked, that will not give bad results "if conjoined with universal idiocy"). In Mill's day, this would not have seemed a noteworthy observation; but today, when we understand that a properly formalized algorithm *must* give the results it is supposed to if

slavishly followed 'even by a moron', as one says, we can
see that Mill was admitting that he had not succeeded in
formalizing inductive logic. If there is an objective sense in
which some inductive inferences by analogy are
'warranted' and others are 'unwarranted', then there must
be an objective sense in which some judgements of what is
'reasonable' are better than others, *even if we cannot give a
general criterion*.

Let us think a little more about Collingwood's inference.
The principle on which he relies (that calling things
'wicked' can make them seem fascinating) seems plausible.
Apart from sexual examples, do we really have so much
data in support of this generalization? Exactly what is it?
Who collected it? Under what conditions?

I do not mean at all to suggest that Collingwood's
psychological generalization is implausible. I think it is
highly plausible. But the high probability I ascribe to it is
not based on a body of properly–collected 'statistical
evidence' (although it is partly based on instances I can
think of, or rather on the *feeling of certainty* that I could
think of such instances if I tried), but on my empathetic
understanding of 'how people work'. In *Meaning and the
Moral Sciences*,[18] I argued that *Verstehen* (empathetic
understanding) *is* methodologically relevant in the social
sciences (that it is, in technical terms, a source of 'prior
probability'). Unless we admit that this is so, we cannot
regard historical reasoning as warranted at all. With this
factor left out, what we have looks like a doubtful analogy
from we-know-not-what-data collected under we-know-not-
what-conditions. Try to 'correct' the defect' by formulating
a 'proper statistical law' supported by 'proper data' and
you are back in the Nagelian dream of 'history as immature
sociology' and 'laws of historical development'.

Nor did I pick an atypical case from which to generalize;
virtually every historical generalization relies on analogies,
and most rely on an empathetic understanding of 'how
people work' as well. Even Marx's Historical Materialism

does so, although Marx was furious when Stirner pointed this out.[19] If one tries, with Ernest Nagel, to simply *assimilate* the inferences we make in history to the inferences of the physicist, the effect is not to show that history is proper 'science' after all, but to make it all look like *terrible* science. And similar points apply to the evidence for and the character of the inferences we *have to make* when we discuss politics, or, for that matter, when we think about the character and dispositions of people we know. . .

One way out of the difficulty might be to supplement the present formal accounts of scientific method by a further set of rules which would determine what analogies are reasonable, which predicates are projectible, what weight we should give to our empathetic intuitions about how people are likely to behave under specified circumstances, and so on. But there does not appear to be any reason to think that such rules would be any simpler than a complete description of the total psychology of an ideally rational human being. (I have even succeeded in using Gödelian arguments[20] to show that if the inductive logic of an 'ideally rational human being' obeys the standard De Finetti-Shimony constraints on 'coherence', then even an ideally rational human being could not discover what the complete computational description of that inductive logic is.) The hope for a formal method, capable of being isolated from our judgements about the nature of the world, seems to have been frustrated. And if we do widen the notion of a method so that a formalization of the complete psychology of an ideally rational human being counts as a 'method', there is no reason to think that a 'method' in this sense must be independent of the human being's judgements about metaphysics, aesthetics, or whatever. The whole reason for believing that the scientific method would not have ethical (or metaphysical) presuppositions was that it was supposed to be a *formal* method, after all.

The 'Epistemological Problem'

If appeals to the 'scientific method' do not solve what
one might call the epistemological problem in ethics or
anywhere else, then what *can* we say about it? What I am
going to say should not be a surprise to anyone who has
followed these lectures. For example, I don't think that one
can short-circuit the entire issue in ethics by saying that
ethical beliefs aren't really *beliefs* but something else, say
'expressions of attitude' or 'speech acts other than saying
what is true or false'. These once popular moves were just
ways of saying that values aren't 'really there', that is,
aren't in 'the things in themselves' but are rather 'mere
projections'. This line *has*, to be sure, a certain
plausibility—it always has, and for the same reason. The
problem with it is not that it doesn't 'work', that it doesn't
succeed in dissolving or evading the problem it is meant to
dissolve or evade, but that it *works too well*. It is, so to
speak, a Universal Solvent for philosophical problems. One
can of course 'get rid of' the whole issue of the
epistemological status of moral beliefs by denying that we
really do say anything that is true or false when we make
moral judgements, and by saying that values are just
'feelings that we project onto the world'. As I pointed out
in the first lecture, one can get rid of the problem of the
existence of mathematical entities in exactly the same way,
by saying that there aren't really any such things, that they
are objects that we merely project onto the world, and that
statements such as 'Every number has a successor', which
seem to assert the existence of an infinite number of
'problematical mathematical entities', are not really true at
all. Simon Blackburn[21] is very fond of this move, and he is
not at all troubled by the fact that on his account science,
which he claims really is about things as they are in
themselves, depends in large part on premises which are
not true at all but are mere 'projections'. One can also get
rid of the problem of how *modal* statements can be true,
that is, how it can be true that certain states of affairs are
'possible', or how something can be 'necessary'. One can

get rid of the problem of how causal statements or counterfactual statements can be true—one can 'solve' just about *any* philosophical problem either by saying that the objects in question don't really exist, or by saying that the statements in question don't really have a truth value. If one is desperate enough or daring enough, one can say that 'truth' itself is a projection (this is, as far as I can understand it, the content of the popular 'disquotational theory of truth'.[22]

On the other hand, rejecting the spectator point of view, taking the agent point of view towards my own moral beliefs, and recognizing that *all* of the beliefs that I find indispensible in life must be treated by me as assertions which are true or false (and which I believe are true), without an invidious distinction between *noumena* and *phenomena*, is not the same thing as lapsing back into metaphysical realism about one's own moral beliefs any more than taking this attitude towards one's beliefs about commonsense material objects or towards causal beliefs or mathematical beliefs means lapsing back into metaphysical realism about commonsense objects, or causality, or mathematical objects/modalities. It also does not require us to give up our pluralism or our fallibilism: one does not have to believe in a unique *best* moral version, or a unique *best* causal version, or a unique *best* mathematical version; what we have are *better and worse* versions, and that *is* objectivity.

Once we have given up the picture of a totality of Noumenal Objects and Properties from which our different conceptual schemes merely make one or another selection, the picture of a Noumenal Dough which our conceptual schemes merely 'slice up' differently, we are forced to recognize with William James that the question as to how much of our web of belief reflects the world 'in itself' and how much is our 'conceptual contribution' makes no more sense than the question:[23] 'Does a man walk more essentially with his left leg or his right'? The trail of the human serpent is over all.

In particular, our moral beliefs, in my view, are not

approximations to The Universe's Own Moral Truths, just
as our scientific beliefs are not approximations to The
Universe's Own Scientific Theory. But I don't conclude
from this that that truth is just a matter of what the folks in
my culture believe. Ruth Anna Putnam[24] has written that
we 'make' facts and we 'make' values; but the fact that we
make facts and values doesn't mean that they are arbitrary,
or that they can't be better or worse. She compares the
situation to the making of artifacts; we *literally* make
artifacts, and we don't make them according to Nature's
Own Blueprint, nor is there always one design which is
forced upon all designers by Natural Law (when we make
knives, we don't follow The Universe's Own Design for a
Knife), but it doesn't follow that the knives we make don't
satisfy real needs, and knives may certainly be better or
worse.

I think her point well taken. The 'moral images' I talked
about in the last lecture are human creations. The moral
image of civic republicanism or communitarianism, the
moral image of human fraternity, the moral image of
humans as made in God's likeness, and the Kantian moral
image of the Kingdom of Ends, or of Self-Legislating
agents, are all human creations. But that doesn't mean that
the statements we make, using the language of one or
another such moral image, cannot be right or wrong. The
fact that they are human creations does mean, however,
that in principle they can be superseded, merged,
combined, and so on—all of the operations on 'versions'
that Nelson Goodman describes in his deep little book[25] on
'worldmaking' apply also to the making of moral worlds.

Let me come back to Ruth Anna Putnam's analogy
between value-making and knife-making, or in my
terminology, between manufacturing moral images and
manufacturing artifacts. There is an obvious objection,
which she is aware of and discusses. Someone might say,
'Yes, you are saying that the values we make, or the moral
images we make, are better or worse. But that supposes
that there are standards for what is a better or what is a
worse. Won't the whole problem of an Epistemology or an
Ontology for moral discourse re-arise when we ask about

the status of these standards?' Any good Goodmanian, or
any good Quinean, should be able to think of the answer to
that one at once. The picture, of course, is that standards
pre-exist, say, standards for making inductive inferences,
or standards for making moral images, or whatever; and
the things we do are to be judged against those pre-existing
canons. But this is just the picture that Goodman attacked
in his famous writing on induction,[26] and that Quine
attacks in his 'naturalized epistemology'. Standards and
practices, pragmatists have always insisted, must be
developed together and constantly revised by a procedure
of delicate mutual adjustment. The standards by which we
judge and compare our moral images are themselves
creations as much as the moral images.

But wait a minute! If this is so, aren't we back in total
Irrationalism? Ruth Anna Putnam, following the line of
John Dewey, appeals at this point to the notion of a *need*.
It is because there are real human needs, and not merely
desires, that it makes sense to distinguish between better
and worse values, and, for that matter, between better and
worse knives. What are these pre-existing human needs
and how are they distinguished from mere desires? Here,
Dewey, like Goodman, tells us that human needs also do
not pre-exist, that humanity is constantly redesigning itself,
and that we *create* needs. Once again, many will feel the
sense of vertigo, or worse, the sense of falling into a
bottomless pit. Our notions—the notion of a value, the
notion of a moral image, the notion of a standard, the
notion of a need—are so intertwined that none of them can
provide a 'foundation' for ethics. That, I think, is exactly
right. We must come to see that there is no possibility of a
'foundation' for ethics, just as we have come to see that
there is no possibility of a 'foundation' for scientific
knowledge, or for any other kind of knowledge.

I would like to close by illustrating our position with the
aid of an analogy, but to draw the analogy I must take the
risk of forgetting the question that we have been
discussing, the question of ethics and of the 'justification'
of moral images. Yet there is a reason for what may look
like an abrupt change of subject at the very end of my

lectures. We are haunted by a certain culturally-accepted distinction between 'science' and 'ethics', but we are also haunted by another culturally-accepted distinction, the distinction between 'absolute' and 'instrumental' values— in effect, the distinction between valuing and *engineering*. Kant himself was in the grip of this dichotomy when he insisted that all 'imperatives' must be either 'hypothetical' or 'categorical'. The assumption has always been that 'hypothetical imperatives', statements about what one ought to do *if* one wants to attain a particular end, are unproblematic in exactly the way that scientific statements are thought to be unproblematic. My purpose in my concluding remarks will be to show that this is wrong; that if we are in a position that seems troubling in 'ethics', we are in exactly the same position in 'engineering', that the hypothetical imperative is in the same situation as the categorical, that rationality is as difficult a thing to 'explain' in both cases.

The case I wish to discuss is one that Peirce used to draw a certain connection between scientific problems and ethical problems—though not the one I wish to draw. In my opinion, Peirce's great contribution lies in his perception of the depth of individual problems, even if he did not succeed in building a unified system out of all those wonderful perceptions. One of these great flashes of genius occurs when Peirce discusses the question, Why should a person do what is most *likely* to work?

Suppose I am in a situation in which I have to do X or Y and the probability of success is very high if I do X and very low if I do Y. We can put Peirce's question this way: Why should I do X? Why is the fact that X will probably succeed a reason to do it?

The Importance of Peirce's Puzzle

Many philosophers would say that the reason one should be guided by the probabilities is that the *frequency of successes* one will enjoy will be higher if one does so.

Observe that the case is not one in which the probabilities themselves are at all uncertain; we are supposed to know the probabilities, and so the problem of induction, that is, the problem of ascertaining the probabilities, is not the issue here. The issue is that we know the probability of success is high if one does X, low if one does Y, and the question is why should we do X? Observe also that the given knowledge is of precisely the type that is supposed to 'justify' the hypothetical imperative 'Do X if you want success'.

It is at this point in the argument that Peirce's genius shows itself. Suppose that I am an old man, or that for some other reason I don't believe I have many years of life ahead of me. What do beliefs about what my success-frequency would be if I *were* to live a long time and be involved in a great many of these situations have to do with what I should do in this *one* situation? In fact, Peirce considers a situation in which the choice is between 'eternal felicity' and 'everlasting woe'. By the very nature of this situation, there isn't going to *be* any *further* 'gambling situation' which the rational agent will have to deal with. Specifically, Peirce's thought example is this:[27] one has to choose between two arrangements. Each arrangement is probabilistic; under each arrangement, one will select a card from a well-shuffled pack with 25 cards in it, one of which is specially designated. The outcome depends in both cases on whether or not one draws the specially designated card. Under arrangement A, one gets everlasting woe if one draws the designated card and eternal felicity if one draws any other card, so that one's chances of eternal felicity are twenty-four to one; while under the second arrangement it is the other way around—one gets eternal felicity if one draws the designated card and everlasting woe if one draws any other card, so that one's chances of everlasting woe are twenty-four to one. (Those for whom the notion of immortality is troubling can substitute 'an easy death' and 'a hard death' for eternal felicity and everlasting woe, respectively.) We *all* believe that a rational person would choose arrangement A. Peirce's question is *Why should he?*

Reichenbach held that probability statements about the single case are simply a *fictitious transfer* of relative frequencies in the long run,[28] or of knowledge of relative frequencies in the long run. Notice that this is yet another example of the use of the notion of a Projection; Reichenbach was saying that the very statement that Jones will have only one chance in twenty-five of eternal felicity *this one time* under arrangement *B* is a 'projection'. There is no fact about the single unrepeatable situation which is *the fact that choice* A *gives Jones twenty-four chances out of twenty-five of eternal felicity.* (Recently, Stephen Leeds has written a stimulating paper[29] arguing that the whole notion of probability is a Projection.)

Peirce's problem comes out very clearly if we take the view that probability just is relative frequency in the long run. The person in the situation knows a fact which is *utterly irrelevant* to what he should do. He knows that *if there were* a series of situations like this one, then he *would have* eternal felicity twenty-four times out of every twenty-five if he were to choose arrangement *A* each time. But a person can have eternal felicity or everlasting woe only once! His problem is not how to achieve eternal felicity twenty-four times *out of every twenty-five*; his problem is to obtain eternal felicity *this* time. Why should he pick arrangement *A*?

The only answer we can give is that it is more probable that he will have eternal felicity under arrangement *A*. But the question was, remember, Why should one *expect* what is *probable*? If you say that you should expect what is *probable* because it is *likely* to happen this time, you're not answering the question, you're just, as it were, repeating the advice: *Expect what is probable.* If you say, 'Well, it's *reasonable* to expect what is probable,' well—in this situation, isn't 'reasonable' just a synonym for 'probable', in the Keynes-Carnap sense of 'logical probability'? Isn't 'It's reasonable to expect what is probable to happen,' just another way of saying 'It's *probable* (in the logical sense of probability) that what will probably happen (in the frequency sense of probability) will happen in any individual case (unless we know of some respect in which the individual case is atypical)?

We are forced back, then, to the view that a reasonable person adjusts his expectations to the *logical* probability; and this time, any beliefs we may have about how this will lead us to fare in the long run are seen to be irrelevant to the problem. That there is such a thing as the 'logical probability', that it corresponds to the frequency in a long series (if there *were* a long series), and that a reasonable person adjusts his beliefs to *it* become just Ultimate Logical (*read*: metaphysical) Facts.

Peirce's own solution to this problem is one of the sources of inspiration for the views of Apel and Habermas that I mentioned in the last lecture. According to Peirce, one can *only* be rational if one *identifies* himself psychologically with a whole ongoing—in fact, a potentially infinite—community of investigators. It is only because I care about what *might* happen to people in similar situations that I do what has the best *chance* in my own situation. My belief that *I* in this one *unrepeatable* situation am somehow more likely to experience eternal felicity than eternal woe is fundamentally, then, just what Reichenbach said it was, a fictitious transfer, on Peirce's view. What is true, and not fiction or projection, however, is that my fellows, the members of the community with which I identify, will have eternal felicity twenty-four times out of twenty-five if they follow this strategy; or more generally, even if this one particular situation is never repeated, that if in all the various *uncorrelated* cases of this kind or any other kind that they find themselves in they always follow the probabilities, then in the long run they will experience more successes and fewer losses.

But can it really be that the reason I would choose arrangement *A* is that I am *altruistic*? Maybe I am, but isn't it obvious that I would choose arrangement *A* first and foremost because it would avoid everlasting woe *in my own case*? Peirce's argument is that I ought to choose arrangement *A* for what one might describe as 'Rule Utilitarian' reasons: in choosing this arrangement I am supporting, and helping to perpetuate, a rule which will benefit mankind (or the community of rational investigators) *in the long run*. Is this really what is in my mind when what I am facing is *torture* ('everlasting woe')? Frankly, it isn't. I cannot give a reason for doing what I would do in this case, if the only reasons allowed are in terms of 'what will happen in the long run if'. And this shows that even in the *means-end* kind of problem, I must fall back on unformalized reason.

Today, many people[30] think that the only reason for being *reasonable* at all is that one will arrive at truth in theory and success in action *more often* if one is reasonable. Some people[31] have even proposed replacing the notion of a 'reasonable' method by the notion of a reliable method: one that, as a matter of fact, leads to successful outcomes with a high relative frequency. Notice that (if you agree with me in finding Peirce's own solution incredible) these approaches are helpless in the face of Peirce's problem. If my *only* reason for believing that I should be reasonable were my beliefs about what will happen *in the long run* if I act or believe reasonably, then I would have absolutely *no* reason (apart from the implausible reason of altruism) to think it better to be reasonable in an unrepeatable single case like the one described. In fact, as I came close to the end of my life, and found myself unable to make many more 'bets', then my reasons for doing what is reasonable or expecting what is reasonable should diminish very sharply, on this view. The fact is that we have an *underived*, a *primitive* obligation of some kind to be reasonable, not a 'moral obligation' or an 'ethical obligation', to be sure, but nevertheless a very real obligation to be reasonable, which—contrary to Peirce—is *not* reducible to my expectations about the long run and my interest in the welfare of others or in my own welfare at other times. I *also* believe that it will work better in the long run for people to be reasonable, certainly; but when the question is *Why do you expect that, in this* unrepeatable *case, what is extremely likely to happen will happen?*, here I have to say with Wittgenstein: 'This is where my spade is turned. This is what I do, this is what I say.'

My reason for bringing this up when the question was what to do about the 'bottomless pit' phenomenon in ethics, with our concern about the lack of a Foundation in ethics, is that in the case just described—a case which has to do with reasonableness about 'means and ends', rather than with ethics—my epistemic situation is exactly the same. I do think, and I think it warranted to think, that 'acting on the probabilities' is the only rational thing to do, and that one ought to do the rational thing even in unrepeatable situations. In the ethical case, I do think, and I think it warranted to think, that a person who has a sense of human brotherhood is better than a person who lacks a sense of human brotherhood. A person who is capable of thinking for himself about how to live is better than a person who has lost or never developed the capacity to think for himself about how to live; but, whether the question be about single-case probability or about ethics, I don't *know how I know* these things. These are cases in which I find that I have to say: "I have reached bedrock and this is where my spade is turned."[32]

Recognizing that there are certain places where one's spade is turned; recognizing, with Wittgenstein, that there are places where our explanations run out, isn't saying that any particular place is *permanently* fated to be 'bedrock', or that any particular belief is forever immune from criticism. This is where my spade is turned *now*. This is where my justifications and explanations stop *now*. To recognize that a loyal human being is better than a disloyal human being, that a person capable of *philia* is better than a person incapable of *philia*, that a person capable of a sense of community, of citizenship in a *polis*, is better than a person who is incapable of a sense of community or of citizenship in a *polis*, and so forth, is not to say that any one of these values or any one of the moral pictures which may lie behind and organize these values is final, in the sense, of being exclusively or exhaustively correct. Our moral images are in a process of development and reform.

But it is to say that at each stage in that development and reform, there will be places, many places, at which we have to say: 'This is where my spade is turned.'

None of this goes against the idea that rational criticism of a moral vision is possible. A moral vision may contradict, for example, what we know or think it rational to believe on other grounds, be they logical, metaphysical, or empirical. But we cannot any longer hope that these kinds of criticism will leave just *one* moral vision intact. Ultimately, there is still a point at which one has to say: 'This is where my spade is turned.'

This is *not* Feyerabendian Relativism. It *is* a rejection of the project of Epistemology with a capital 'E'. In the first lecture I tried to show that rejecting the project of Ontology—of a description of things as they are 'apart from our conceptual systems'—does not put an end to all the interesting questions about language and thought; rather it calls attention to phenomena we have been downplaying (when we do not actually ignore them), for example, the phenomenon I called conceptual relativity. And similarly, rejecting the project of Epistemology with a capital 'E'—the project of a Universal Method for telling who has 'reason on his side' no matter *what* the dispute—will not put an end to all the interesting questions about knowledge in science and in ethics; instead it will direct our attention to other phenomena we have been trying to ignore (for example, the analogies between epistemological problems—note the small 'e'—connected with science and epistemological problems connected with values). Above all, I hope it may redirect philosophical energy to one of its very traditional tasks—the one task philosophy should never abandon—the task of providing meaningful, important, and discussable images of the human situation in the world.

NOTES

Notes to Lecture I
(pages 3–21)

[1]*Science, Perception, and Reality*, Atlantic Highlands, NJ: Humanities Press, 1963.

[2]*The Crisis of the European Sciences and Transcendental Phenomenology*, translated by David Carr, Evanston: Northwestern University Press, 1970.

[3]See C. L. Hardin's 'Are "Scientific" Objects Colored?', in *Mind*, XCIII, No. 22 (October 1964), 491-500.

[4]The commonsense notion of 'solidity' should not be confused with the physicist's notion of being in 'the solid state'. For example, a sand dune is in the 'solid state' but is not solid in the ordinary sense of the term, while a bottle of milk may be solid, but most of its contents are not in the solid state.

[5]"The "Mental" and the "Physical"', in *Minnesota Studies in the Philosophy of Science*, vol. II, *Concepts, Theories and the Mind–Body Problem*, ed. by Feigl, Scriven, and Maxwell, Minneapolis: University of Minnesota Press,1958, 370-497.

[6]This is argued in my *Representation and Reality*, Montgomery, Vt: Bradford Books, forthcoming.

[7]D. C. Dennett, *Content and Consciousness*, Atlantic Highlands, NJ: Humanities Press, 1969.

[8]*Philosophy and the Mirror of Nature*, Princeton: Princeton University Press, 1979.

[9]Stephen Stich, *From Folk Psychology to Cognitive Science: The Case Against Belief*, Cambridge, Ma: M.I.T. Press, 1983.

[10]'On What There Is', reprinted in *From a Logical Point of View*, Cambridge, Ma: Harvard 1953.

[11]White has advocated doing this early and late (*Toward Reunion in Philosophy*, Cambridge, Ma: Harvard University Press, 1956; *What Is and What Ought to Be Done*, Oxford: Oxford University Press, 1981).

Notes to Lecture II
(pages 23–40)

[1]As explained in the Preface, this 'lecture' was not actually read in Washington.

[2]In logic a way of connecting statements is called 'truth functional' if the truth value of the resulting statement can be determined given just the truth values of the components. Counterfactual conditionals all have false antecedants and typically they have false consequents as well; yet some of them are true and some false. Thus the counterfactual is not a truth–function of its parts.

[3]David Lewis, *Counterfactuals*, Cambridge, Ma: Harvard University Press, 1973.

[4]This idea was implicit in Carnap's treatment of dispositional predicates via "reduction sentences" in 'Testability and Meaning', *Philosophy of Science*, 3:420–468 (1936); 4:1–40 (1937).

[5]J.L. Mackie, *The Cement of the Universe*, New York, Oxford University Press, 1974.

[6]E.g., Hempel proposed to count as complete "explanations" only those explantions which fit his strict Deductive Nomological Model. (Cf. Hempel and Oppenheim, 'The Logic of Scientific Explanation', reprinted in Feigl and Brodbeck (eds), *Readings in the Philosophy of Scienc*, 319-352, New York: Appleton-Century-Crofts, 1953.

[7]Mackie referred to the notion we use in these as our "paleolithic" notion of causation. See n. 5.

Notes to Lecture III
(pages 41–62)

[1]The picture presented in the second Critique (and at times, unfortunately, in the first) is, in many ways, a reversion to Kant's picture in the *Prolegomena* in which the noumenal world simply *is* the world, the world as it is 'in itself', and the world of experience is the world of Lockean 'secondary qualities'—or, rather, what that world would become if we said that extension, and, indeed, all the qualities we know by scientific or ordinary perceptual means are 'secondary' in Locke's sense.

[2]In some versions, 'provided they do not forfeit this right by doing some serious evil' would be inserted as a qualification here.

[3]See Rawls's *A Theory of Justice*, Cambridge, Ma: Harvard University Press, 1971, and his Dewey Lectures, 'Kantian Constructivism in Moral Theory', which occupied an entire volume of *The Journal of Philosophy*, vol. LXXVII, number 9, September 1980.

[4]*After Virtue*, Notre Dame: University of Notre Dame Press, 1980.

[5]*Grundlegung*, Zweiter Abschnitt 418ff. Translated as *The Fundamental*

Principles of the Metaphysic of Morals, translated by Thomas K. Abbott,
New York: Liberal Arts Press, 1949; *vide* Second Section, 35ff, e.g., "But
unfortunately the notion of happiness is so indefinite that although
every man wishes to attain it, yet he can never say definitely and
consistently what it is that he really wishes and wills."

[6]Compare Rawls's Dewey Lectures, cited in n.3.

[7]Dieter Henrich's lectures on Kant's Transcendental Deduction at
Harvard are the source for this.

[8]"Moral image of the world" comes from Dieter Henrich's Kant lectures
at Harvard.

[9]P.F. Strawson, *The Bounds of Sense*, London: Methuen, 1966.

[10]Jürgen Habermas, *Knowledge and Human Interests*, translated by
Jeremy J. Shapiro, Boston: Beacon Press, 1971.

[11]Karl-Otto Apel, *Charles S. Peirce, from Pragmatism to Pragmaticism*,
translated by John Michael Krois, Amherst: University of Massachusetts
Press, 1981.

[12]This egalitarianism was not always a part of Utilitarian doctrine,
however. "Each is to count for one, none for more than one" was
Bentham's addition: Hutcheson, who anticipated Bentham with a
hedonic calculus, operated with the idea that "the Dignity, or moral
importance of persons, may compensate Numbers"—i.e., some people
who were more important were to count for more.

Lecture IV
(pages 63–86)

[1]*Reason, Truth, and History*, New York: Cambridge University Press,
1981.

[2]Cf. *The Methodology of the Social Sciences*, New York: The Free Press
(MacMillan), 1949.

[3]For example, the *shape* of an object depends on the velocity of the
observer relative to the object, in the Special Theory of Relativity.
'Square' is, thus, strictly speaking, a *frame-dependent* term in relativity
physics. This illustrates the fact that no term in the ordinary
'observation vocabulary' of the physicist is immune from the possibility
of receiving extremely complex kinds of theoretical loading.

[4]See *The Structure of Scientific Revolutions*, Chicago: University of
Chicago Press, 1981.

[5]Henri Pirenne, *Mohammed and Charlemagne* (translation of his
Mahomet et Charlemagne), Totawa, NJ: Barnes and Noble, 1980.

[6]See C.G. Hempel's classic paper, 'Problems and Changes in the
Empiricist Criterion of Meaning', in *Revue International de Philosophie*,
4:41-63 (1950), reprinted in L. Linsky, ed., *Semantics and the
Philosophy of Language*, pp. 163–85, Urbana: University of Illinois
Press, 1952.

[7]E.g., Nagel wrote that "There appears to be no good reason for claiming

that the general pattern of explanations in historical inquiry . . . differs from those encountered in the generalizing and the natural science" ('The Logic of Historical Analysis', in H. Feigl and M. Brodbeck (eds), *Readings in the Philosophy of Science*, New York: Appleton-Century-Crofts, 1953, 688–700.) Immediately after making this statement, Nagel goes on to say that the "explanatory premises in history" include laws "as well as many explicitly (although incompletely) formulated statements of initial conditions". Note that 'law' and 'initial conditions' are physicists' jargon, and not any historian's way of speaking.

[8]E.g., Reichenbach writes that "The argument that sociological happenings are unique and do not repeat themselves breaks down because the same is true for physical happenings. The weather of one day is never the same as that of another day. The condition of one piece of wood is never the same as that of any other piece of wood. The scientist overcomes these difficulties by incorporating the individual cases into a class and looking for laws that control the unique conditions at least in a majority of cases. Why should the social scientist be unable to do the same thing?" *The Rise of Scientific Philosophy*, Berkeley: University of California Press, 1951, 309–310.

[9]See, for example, *Experience and Prediction*, Chicago: University of Chicago Press, 1938.

[10]Richard Boyd has recently argued this point of view in (unpublished at this writing) lectures at the University of California and elsewhere.

[11]For example, the factual statement that the world is more than 6,000 years old does not have the property of being provable to every intelligent person—I recently came across an article by Paul Rosenbloom—the author of the book on advanced mathematical logic that I worked through in my graduate student days—defending his right to believe that God created the world less than 6,000 years ago. Rosenbloom's claim is that God may have created the world at the time traditional Judaism gives as the moment of Creation, but complete with monuments, written records, people with false memories, etc., as in the familiar sceptical hypothesis about 'the world coming into existence five minutes ago'.

[12]The reference was to Quine's claim (in *Word and Object*) that talk of meaning (and in the case of an alien language, even of truth and reference) belongs to our 'second class conceptual system'; the one we use when our interests are 'heuristic' or practical. The 'first class' conceptual system, Quine says, is the conceptual system of physics. This is what describes "the true and ultimate nature of reality".

[13]See *Reason, Truth and History*, pp.105–113.

[14]E.g., in *The Rise of Scientific Philosophy* (Chapter 17).

[15]Chapter 8, op. cit.

[16]The argument depends on the existence of 'non-projectible predicates'. Cf. Goodman's *Fact, Fiction and Forecast*, 4th edition, Harvard, 1983, with foreward by H. Putnam. For a discussion of the significance of Goodman's result see my foreword to this edition and my *Reason, Truth and History*, 193ff.

[17]*The Theory of Probability* (English Translation), second edition, p.450, Berkeley: University of California Press, 1949.

[18]London: Routledge and Kegan Paul, 1978.

[19]Marx explains the *origin* of exploitation by pointing out that with the division of (mental from manual) labor there appeared an opportunity for the mental workers to exploit the manual workers. Stirner pointed out that there is a hidden psychological premiss (one that Marx did not want to admit), namely that *if people are in a position to exploit other people, they tend to do so*. Rather than proposing a less disagreeable psychological premiss, in *The German Ideology* Marx simply asserts: "I need no psychological premisses. Exploitation *issues directly* from the division of labor" (sic).

[20]Cf. my 'Reflexive Reflections', in *Epistemology, Methodology and Philosophy of Science, Essays in Honour of Carl G. Hempel on the Occasion of his 80th Birthday*, W.K. Essler, H. Putnam, and W. Stegmüller, Dordrecht: Reidel, 1985, 143–154. This Festschrift was also published as vol. 22, Nos. 1, 2, and 3 (January 1985) of *Erkenntnis*, with the same pagination.

[21]Cf. Blackburn's *Spreading the Word*, Oxford: Clarendon, 1984, especially Chapter 6.

[22]See my 'On Truth', in *How Many Questions, essays in honor of Sidney Morgenbesser*, Leigh S. Cauman et al (eds.), Indianapolis: Hackett, 1983, 35–56.

[23]James' seventh Lecture on Pragmatism, 'Pragmatism and Humanism', in *Pragmatism and the Meaning of Truth*, Cambridge, Ma: Harvard University press, 1978, pp. 115–130.

[24]'Creating Facts and Values', *Philosophy*, vol. 60, April 1985.

[25]*Ways of Worldmaking*.

[26]*Fact, Fiction and Forecast*

[27]Peirce discusses this example in 'The Doctrine of Chances', p. 69, reprinted in *Chance, Love and Logic*, Morris R. Cohen (ed), New York: Hartcourt, Brace, 1923.

[28]Reichenbach discusses the single case in *The Theory of Probability*, 372ff.

[29]Cf. Leeds's 'Chance, Realism, Quantum Mechanics', *Journal of Philosophy*, 81 (1984), pp. 97–107.

[30]For a discussion of this kind of 'epistemic utilitarianism' see Roderick Firth's presidential address, 'Epistemic Merit, Intrinsic and Instrumental', in *Proceedings and Adresses of the American Philosophical Society*, Sept. 1981, vol. 55, Number 1, 5–23.

[31]For a sophisticated version of this view see Alvin I. Goldman, 'What is Justified Belief?', in George Pappas (ed), *Justification and Knowledge*, Dordrecht: London, 1979.

[32]*Philosophical Investigations*, Oxford: Blackwell, 1953, sec. 217. That Wittgenstein here uses the first person—where my spade is turned—is very important; yet many interpreters try to see his philosophy as one of simple deference to some 'form of life' determined by a community. On this, see also Stanley Cavell's discussion in *The Claim of Reason*, esp. Part One, Chapter V, 'The Natural and The Conventional'.

INDEX